GRAND STAND

Designing Stands for Trade Fairs and Events

N°6

FRAME

CONTENT

CHIP

IN

User experience at
the centre of design

BEN VAN BERKEL, Founder and Principal Architect at UNStudio, talks about the office's approach to stand design and the role of visitor experience strategies in the advancement of the field.

Els Zweerink

'Entertainment for entertainment's sake won't convey the message'

Stand design is not the type of project for which UNStudio is known. How do these projects relate to the studio's extensive body of work? You are right that we are known more for our buildings than for stand design, but in fact these kind of projects enable us to test out materials, construction techniques, finishes, and new spatial and conceptual ideas in a very small space of time. These can then be applied to larger building projects.

What are the main challenges of this type of temporary spatial design when compared to architectural endeavours? The challenges are more specific. On the one hand a stand has to attract attention, it has to stand out and very precisely represent a specific brand or new material using mostly only one large gesture. In stand design for new materials you also have to push the potential of the materials to the limit in order to demonstrate their most important characteristics, whether that be strength, durability, versatility, or a mix of any of these. At the same time, the design has to operate as a very functional, usually small-scale, space.

Talking more specifically about experience-driven stand designs, what do you think are the most effective ways of turning visitors into participants in these spaces? Interaction. The audience needs to participate actively and you have to create the desire for them to do so. You have to engender curiosity to capture their attention and participation in the first place, but then you have to fascinate in order to maintain that attention. The levels of this engagement differ of course depending on the nature of the event: the audience of a trade fair is different to that of a fair that attracts a broader demographic of the public, so you have to get the levels of desired interaction right. For example, for an industry fair showcasing new materials, you need to create spatial experiences that demonstrate the product at its best, while for a stand or installation during an event like Salone del Mobile, you need to completely engage the public in an experience that really means something to them.

What are the advantages and disadvantages of this approach when compared to more passive exhibitions? One advantage is that with more engagement, you can create fascination, which makes communication more direct and optimised. But you have to achieve the right balance: entertaining purely for entertainment's sake, or interaction that isn't designed in a targeted way won't communicate the message you want to get across. There is also the danger of ending up with an interaction overload, as fairs tend to be very extensive and dense and interaction is of course time-consuming. For this reason, moments of more passive viewing can provide a welcome relief and in themselves become a statement.

In _Grand Stand 2_ (Frame, 2008), the proposition was made that, by focusing on user experience, stands could widen the public of trade fairs by making them more inviting events, which would in turn contribute to broadening the discipline of stand design. What is your take on the effect of user experience-driven approaches to the wider trade fair and international exhibition fields? I agree that developing new approaches to user experience can certainly contribute to broadening the discipline of stand design, but when it comes to widening the public, I think this applies more to international exhibition events. Trade fairs are very specific and I believe will remain so, whether user experience is incorporated or not. For such events interactive experiences are more about improving your message to an already professionally engaged public and creating genuine interest and engagement with what you are showcasing.

In the end, trade fairs are commercial events and companies have to invest a lot to participate. We should avoid that the fair becomes a fairground, because some events are not necessarily going to benefit from a wider audience.

Do you think technologies like virtual or augmented reality can render trade fairs obsolete? No, I don't believe so, for a number of reasons. Trade fairs provide a platform for very specific-themed exhibitions. They bring together relevant products and services in a very convenient, focused and condensed way. Virtual and augmented reality can certainly enable the demonstration of the potential of products, materials and concepts in a way that isn't physically possible in the often confined spaces of the fairs, but they don't yet adequately replace reality or the need to see, touch and feel in order to truly experience a product. These events are of course also a platform for companies to make direct connections with interested parties, potential customers and other parties in their field. Direct contact is essential to fairs but, as yet, not a facet of these technologies.

Roman Thomas

Three companies create a symbiotic vision of the future of retail in an installation by STUDIO JOANNA LAAJISTO

DUSSELDORF – With conventional brick-and-mortar stores giving way to online sales, new physical retail concepts have sought to offer consumers a holistic experience rather than simply a point of sale. Affiliated companies Ansorg, Vitra and Vizona joined forces to present their stake in this trend at EuroShop 2017 with an ambitious, large-scale collaborative effort designed and realised by the studio of Finnish designer Joanna Laajisto.

Entitled The Village, the stand comprised an immersive retail environment recalling a Californian outdoor mall. The main atrium featured a plaza-like café, inviting visitors to stop and experience the space as a social, leisurely destination beyond just shopping. Five retail concepts flanked this area, each embodying a fictitious brand in a specific sector: automotive, consumer electronics, health and beauty, fashion, and food. These spaces invited customers into an imagined, comprehensive brand history and retail experience.

The three companies existed symbiotically in the store designs, with Vitra's retail products illuminated by Ansorg's lighting solutions and displayed by Vizona's shop fittings, thus illustrating their versatility across different market sectors and brand identities. A small annex to the space functioned as a 'behind the scenes' workshop where visitors could discover how the companies' individual products were implemented in each space.

1

GRAND STAND 6

1   The food concept presented itself more as a
    neighbourhood meeting place than a simple
    grocery store, mixing vibrant design and texture
    with intuitive merchandise presentation.

2   Sepio, the health and beauty concept, featured
    lighting designed to accentuate skin and make-
    up, and incorporated monitors that offered easy
    access to the complete product range.

3   Flexible display systems allowed the gallery-like
    space of the fashion concept to adapt to the
    accelerated pace of trends in the industry.

Fictitious brand spaces invite customers into an imagined, comprehensive retail experience

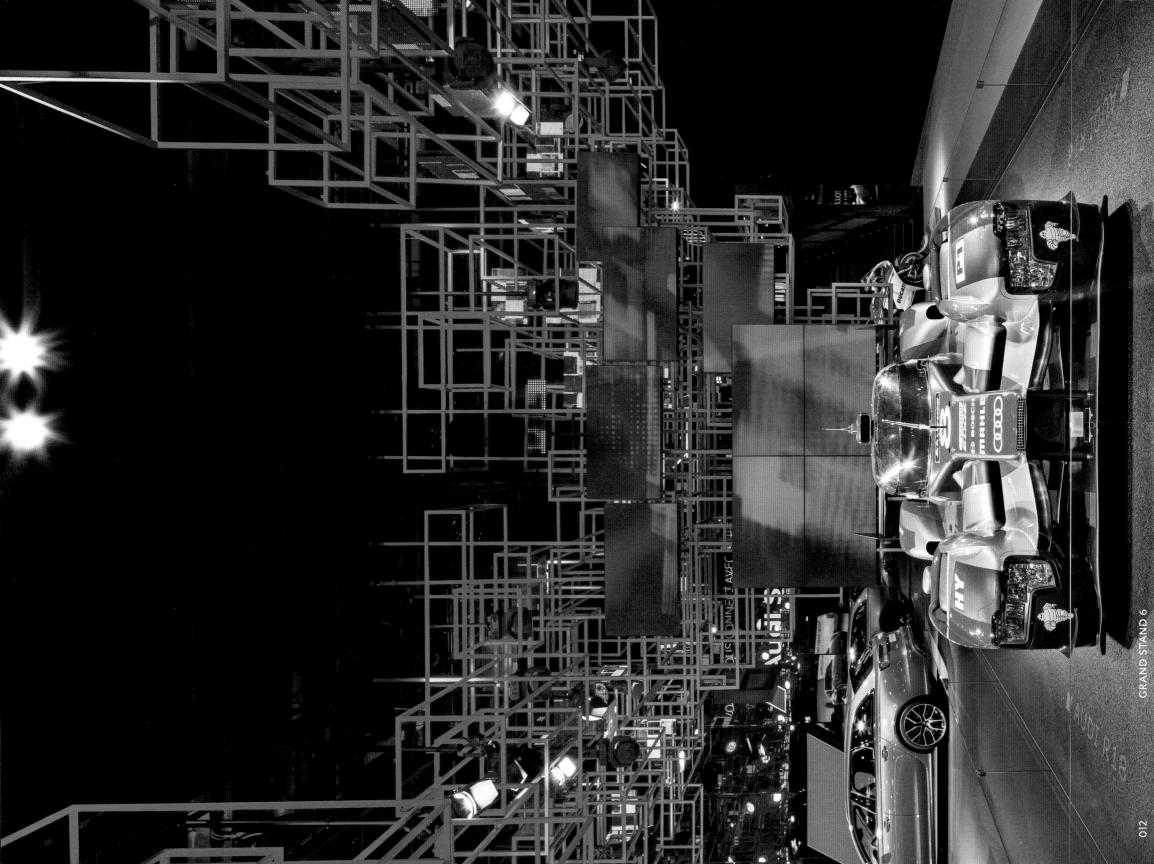

The 'cloud' installation included approximately 7000 processed LED tiles that required significant work in implementation for the interplay of different media.

AUDI

MUTABOR and SCHMIDHUBER create an interactive cloud that guides users through a tailored presentation

PARIS – With digital networking having a greater impact than ever on mobility and transportation, Audi wanted to ensure it created a lasting impression on visitors of the 2016 Paris Motor Show by expressing its alignment with this trend. Realised by Schmidhuber and Mutabor, the stand for the world premiere of the Audi Q5 and Audi RS 3 Limousine was the brand's first completely digital interactive exhibition space.

A ceiling installation over the 2000 m² exhibition area, known as the 'cloud', comprised a framework of 220 modular cube constructions equipped with media-ready surfaces. 'The stand is designed as a media grid,' Schmidhuber explains, 'it serves as a multimedia space that visitors can activate via their smartphones.' Indeed, the space's architecture came to life as visitors interacted with the data streams and various touchpoints allowed them to generate tailor-made information which they could then receive on their smartphones.

These interactions were managed by the Audi Experience Pass, an application developed specially for the stand by Mutabor. Prospective attendees of the exhibit downloaded the application in advance to their devices and were led to the Audi booth as soon as they arrived at the fair. Once inside, the interface guided the user from one touchpoint to the next via push messages which, thanks to NFC technology, resulted in personalised interactions.

KING GEORGE invites
brands to join the circus
with a special installation

Guy Obijn

KORTRIJK — King George proved nothing less than its slogan as a 'mad creative agency' when it was approached by the Biennale Interieur to conceive an installation for its 2016 edition that would break the rules of traditional trade fair exhibitions. Playing on the idea of the theatrical aspect of design, the Belgian studio created an extravagant, circus-themed concept in which various brands were invited to give presentations.

A grand circus tent was erected in the parking lot next to the existing convention building. Ten sea containers extended out from around the tent to provide spaces for the individual brand exhibitions. The brands — an industry-spanning roster that included reputable names such as Marcel Wanders, Duravit, Niko and Cosentino — faced the challenge of devising original product showcases while corresponding thematically with the larger setting.

At the centre of the tent, an octagonal bar covered in angular black and white patterns served as a dynamic meeting point and even offered popcorn to complete the circus theme. During the evenings, a gate could close off the circus from the fair, allowing the participating companies to hold business-to-business events. More than just a display of products, The Circus provided both visitors and brands an unique experience.

'From invitations, to websites and execution, everything was branded in a circus theme: an experience event which was coming to town,' the agency says.

Annika Feuss

BMEL

SIMPLE gives an important public service announcement on nutrition through a light, entertaining and easily-digestible space

COLOGNE – In Form is a nationwide initiative from Germany's Federal Ministry of Food and Agriculture that promotes the importance of healthy eating and exercise. To energise this serious topic, the government body wanted a light, flexible and fun presentation for the campaign's presence at trade fairs, with one notable stop being the 2016 Didacta show.

With a well-known inclination for immersive and entertaining displays, design studio Simple took on this project. The result: a modular and interactive discourse with nutrition and physical activity. The stand immediately catches the visitors' eye with a surreal assortment of inflatable fruits and vegetables. These are suspended from a traverse system, forming a playful backdrop for the stylised contours of the campaign's title.

Further giant foodstuffs served as seating and tables. Accompanying arrows embodied the motion of exercise and gave the food a trajectory toward a giant, semi-transparent shopping basket. This communicated the idea that nutrition begins with conscious consumption. Floor markings transformed the raised wooden floor into an athletic court and created a dynamic activity space that hosted everything from basketball to Zumba.

A hazy installation by **C&C DESIGN** expresses
clear ecological and social messages

GUANGZHOU – Though visually mesmerising, C&C Design's ethereal installation for Guangzhou Design Week 2015, titled Haze, grew from strong politically and socially charged messages in relation to both its local and global contexts. Designer Peng Zheng used a structure of gradient laminated glass to create a feeling of nothingness, an ego death intended to instil a civic and externally oriented mind-set in the visitors.

The installation took the form of an irregular asterisk, whose arms were enclosed glass boxes expanding from the centre at different heights and lengths. The structure's walls changed from transparent to translucent as they approached the floor, creating an effect akin

to its title, and some displayed video projections. Like the virtual world of these projected images, the outside world that lay beyond the walls was visible but inaccessible to visitors, who had to retrace their steps in order to exit the installation.

The experience of the translucent glass world inside had immediate ecological implications, recalling the haze of air pollution that currently plagues major cities in China, including Guangzhou. As well as evoking this ecological concern, the design also looked to draw attention to the 'haze' of social media and e-commerce which obscures one's view of the real world.

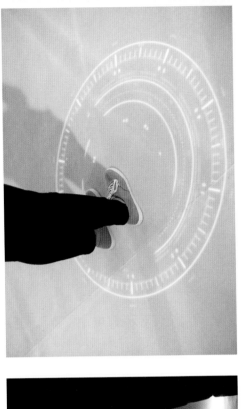

On the third day of the exhibition, visitors were offered a brush to paint graffiti on the glass walls as a means of expressing their interpretation of the project.

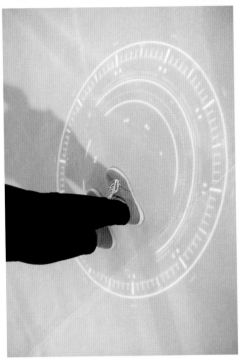

A transparent to translucent gradient creates an effect akin to the installation's title

DART captures the elusive nature of the creative moment of inspiration

D'ART DESIGN GRUPPE

DUSSELDORF — Neuss-based design studio D'art Design Gruppe sought to reconstruct concretely the moment of inspiration in the creative process for its presentation at EuroShop 2017. Taking 'from scratch' as its theme, the firm created an enticing and elusive spectacle at the fair, where its own identity and methodologies could be experienced and actively engaged with.

Angled, 5-m-high mirrored surfaces formed entrances into the enclosed exhibition area, completely obscuring the interior in reflections of the booth's surroundings. Visitors discovered various interactive stations and visual puzzles as they approached the display, all of which represented ways in which ideas can be generated. One could arrange a cluster of three-

dimensional letters to form words and phrases of their choice, or create drawings on iPads that were transmitted live on a large LED wall. Certain mirrors featured offset characters composing a message that could only be deciphered when viewed from the correct angle.

In contrast to the convoluted spatial and visual experience of the various points of entry, the core of the stand took on a clear, monochrome grey. A wide, geometric table entirely covered in grey felt invited visitors to converse, reflect, or browse interactive presentations of the studio's previous projects. The table was flanked by a large, abstract library interspersed with real books which documented the history of Dart.

An enticing and elusive spectacle allows visitors to actively experience and engage with the studio's identity and methodologies

1

3

2

1 An apparently convoluted spatial arrangement stimulated the attention of visitors to the 228 m² space.

2 Encapsulated by mirrors at various angles, 'visitors were confronted with themselves, exactly like the designer during the creative process,' the designers explain.

3 Permanent reflection, different perspectives and dynamic interactions, all part of the creative process, were beautifully recreated in a stand that epitomises 'thinking out of the box'.

HARTMANNVONSIEBENTHAL

uses surreal nature motifs
to create a vibrant vision for
a holistic digital ecosystem

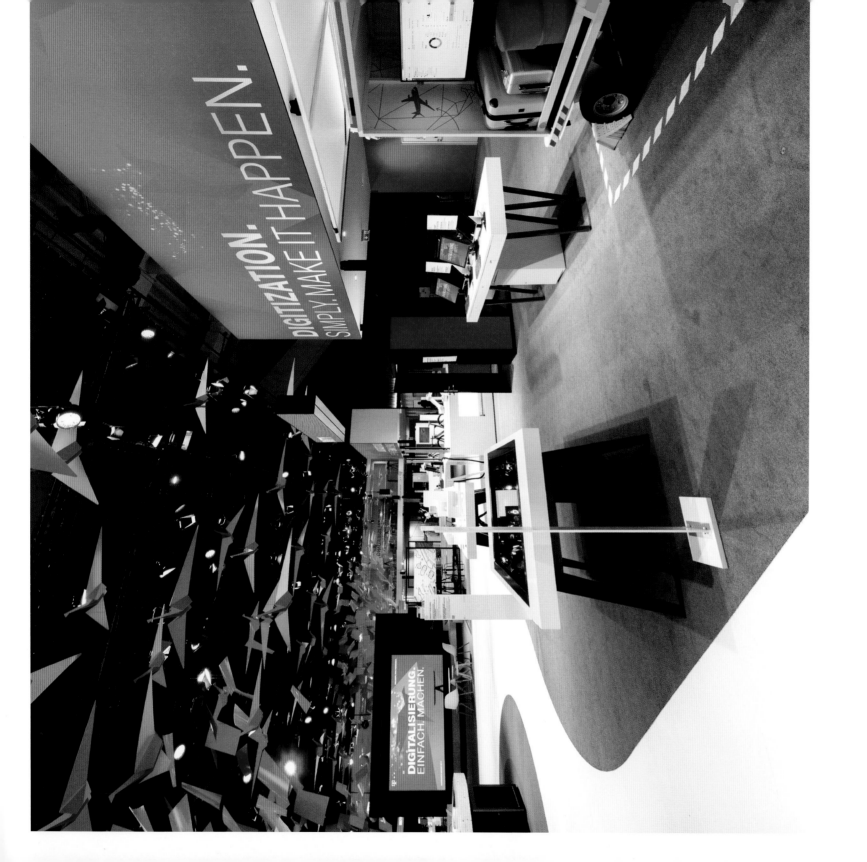

HANNOVER — 'Digitisation. Simply. Make it happen,' read the bright banners of the Deutsche Telekom booth for Hannover Messe 2017. In spite of its brazen heralding of a digital future, the vibrant brand experience created by Berlin-based studio Hartmannvonsiebenthal was inspired by a garden, depicting the company as a fertile ground for innovation and creator of a digital ecosystem.

Natural oak trunks sprouted from the floor up to 5-m-high to form a minimalistic forest. Hanging magenta aluminium elements connected with the colour of the Deutsche Telekom logo and depicted leaves falling from these trees and transforming into flocks of origami birds. The spectacle associated the dynamic development of

the company's technology with the organic, agile motion of nature's forces and metamorphoses. With its expertise in global networks and smart business solutions, Deutsche Telekom also provided a holistic environment for digital life to flourish in both living and working settings.

Work stations interspersing the floor plan offered interactive illustrations of the various contexts in which the company's digital ecosystem could be implemented, from airport logistics and industrial production to virtual reality and energy consumption monitoring. A lounge area on the upper level offered a view out onto the surreal habitat.

The stand offers
interactive illustrations
of the various contexts
in which the company's
digital ecosystem
can be implemented

EPSON

A futuristic café by APOSTROPHYS demonstrates how technology can enhance the physical experience of a product

2

BANGKOK – One of Epson Thailand's main objectives for its 2016 #TrustInYou event was to promote significant improvements to its laser projector technology. Beyond having a new degree of brightness, the projector's enhanced resolution now makes it possible to project onto a small area. Local studio Apostrophys opted to utilise the merits of this new model as a paintbrush in a brand space that integrates visual design, lighting, sound, and new media into a unique experience.

Entitled The Café Tube, the space used small sweets and beverages as a way of demonstrating the smallest possible area for the device's projection mapping. Lasers projected down onto rows of the confections, casting them in radiant, neon hues. Visitors were welcome to partake in four different menus – Summer Rainbow, Winter Freeze, Safari Drink and Galaxtose – which looked to demonstrate the projector's visual quality and at the same time provide a varied and exhilarating visitor experience.

As the latter becomes an ever crescent necessity in the age of e-commerce, the designers predict that the laser projectors will soon become an advertising tool, by offering a means of creating a unique, augmented experience of a product. With Café Tube, the studio claims, the idea was not simply to project the visual onto the food or beverage, but to make the projected visual edible.

1. Larger dynamic projections in the background provided a festive and emotive backdrop to the installation.

2. Products were customised to fit within a 5 cm² radial area, the smallest possible area for the laser's projection mapping.

3. A kinetic wall was activated through image-processing technology, whereby sensors detected the theme of a visitor's beverage cup and projected the corresponding interactive display onto the wall.

Mahassanai Lewchalermwongse

Rath Roongnweangtantisook

Laser projectors offer a means of creating a unique and augmented experience of a product for the consumer

3

UNSTUDIO tackles stress reduction through an experimental, immersive installation

MILAN – Stress has become ever more prevalent among the 'always connected' workforce. The second most frequently reported work-related health problem, it accounts for 50 to 60 per cent of all lost working days in Europe. As part of Salone del Mobile 2017, a collaborative installation between UNStudio and SCAPE, prototyped solutions to this crisis while providing visitors with personalised insight into their own coping mechanisms.

Entitled Reset, the booth comprised three adjacent immersive pods, constructed with light-weight materials and sculpted into a shape and size defined by the human body. The first, an 'intake' pod, fitted visitors with EEG and ECG monitors. Two subsequent spaces allowed the individual user to explore first a passive method of stress

reduction – intimacy – and subsequently, an active method – sound.

A plush environment with fully-cushioned floor and surfaces in the Intimacy pod suggested the secure embrace of the womb. Visitors were allowed to unwind in their most comfortable position, and pulsing lights and ambient heartbeat sounds adapted in real time to their measured heart rate. In contrast, the Sound room encouraged users to interact with the space by playing electric drum pads and discovering sounds on a touch-enabled wall. As with the Intimacy room, a dynamic atmosphere was modulated through measured user activity. A final space gave the user a Reset Index that evaluated their response to the methods with recommendations for future stress reduction techniques.

reset INTIMACY

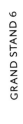

A plush environment with fully-cushioned surfaces suggests the secure embrace of the womb

1 Scientific studies have shown that stress can disrupt cellular communication in the body. The exhibition's sound therapy hence considered whether sending particular frequencies to the user's body could bring cells back into 'tune' with one another.

2 Beyond exploring stress reduction methods, the exhibition also experimented with the concept of 'ambient intelligence'; a system creating an environment unique for and responsive to each user.

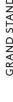

Noe Dewitt

The sparse furnishing of the blacksmith cocktail lounge contrasted with the sensory rapture of the Black Forest room.

EINSZU33
transports visitors to a mystical forest for a unique culinary experience celebrating the history of a home appliances manufacturer

Throughout the experience, mood light and sounds complemented the scenography in order to create a fully immersive experience.

NEW YORK — To commemorate its 333rd year, German high-end appliance giant Gaggenau inaugurated a 3-year series of pop-up concepts around the world with Restaurant 1683, a luxury dining experience to showcase its latest products while celebrating its rich culinary heritage. For a 4-night, invite-only event at the Chelsea Art Beam gallery in New York, studio einszu33 created an immersive, decadent journey through the geographic and socioeconomic origins of the brand.

At the entrance, a floor-to-ceiling, three-dimensional cut-out of a chalet cuckoo clock welcomed the visitors into an experience that started with a cocktail reception styled after an old-fashioned blacksmith shop. An 8-m-long

bar counter made of rough wood boards, dim lighting and a real blacksmith at work, all served to accentuate the fantastical atmosphere of the setting, which formed the backdrop for the company's new EB 333 oven.

Stepping through a black curtain, guests moved to the second space, where mirrors reflecting a full-height waterfall encircled them. A portal in time and space, this passageway led visitors into a multi-sensory representation of the Black Forest, populated by moss, pines and ferns, and animated by the sound of water and birds. In the midst of this tranquil forest, worlds away from the bustling Chelsea streets outside, visitors dined at six stations inspired in the traditional A-frame houses.

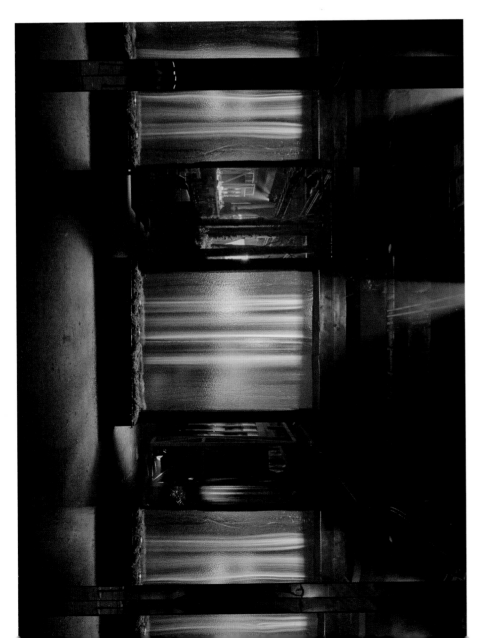

A mirrored waterfall passageway acts as a portal in time and space to the company's Black Forest origins

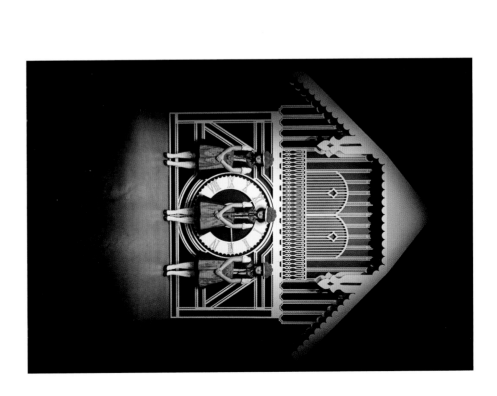

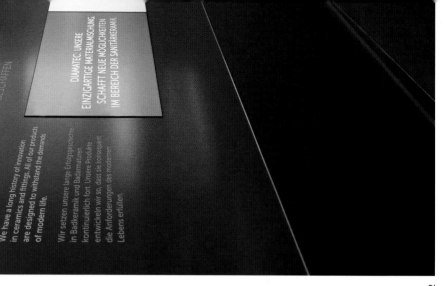

BUILT TO LAST
FÜR HOHE ANFORDERUNGEN GESCHAFFEN

DIAMATEC: UNSERE
EINZIGARTIGE MATERIALMISCHUNG
SCHAFFT NEUE MÖGLICHKEITEN
IM BEREICH DER SANITÄRKERAMIK

We have a long history of innovation
in ceramics and fittings. All of our products
are designed to withstand the demands
of modern life.

Wir setzen unsere lange Erfolgsgeschichte
in Badkeramik und Badarmaturen
kontinuierlich fort. Unsere Produkte
entwickeln wir so, dass sie konsequent
die Anforderungen des modernen
Lebens erfüllen.

Constantin Meyer

IDEAL STANDARD

ISH 2017 visitors step into a stream of innovation with an interactive, multimedia booth by UNIPLAN

1 VR allowed users to explore the Intellimix, a touch-free faucet fitting that saves water with an integrated soap dispenser.

2 The company's AquaBlade, a rimless WC, featured a live demonstration that was synchronised with video content on an LED screen.

FRANKFURT – As part of a new marketing direction for its water management solutions targeted specifically at public and commercial washrooms, Ideal Standard sought to redefine its image at ISH 2017. The international company commissioned Uniplan to turn their new logo and corporate design into a brand architecture that would be more open and captivating than ever to the public.

The clean, purist aesthetic of the main exhibition area, bounded by simple, rectilinear white panels, was interjected by a deep blue, longitudinal corridor, opened at each end and with slit entrances along its lateral walls. Suspended LED stripes ran across this

'innovation stream' like a rapid flow of water, illuminating numerous product exhibits in its path and representing the innovative force of Ideal Standard.

The displays were divided into four key product areas – fittings, wash basins, WCs and shower tubs – each utilising interactive multimedia and dynamic installations to demonstrate their integration with a smart, interconnected world. For example, a transparent LED screen superimposed over the company's EasyBox system directly overlaid product information in a real wall mounting setting, while VR headsets allowed visitors to visualise possible uses and environments for other products.

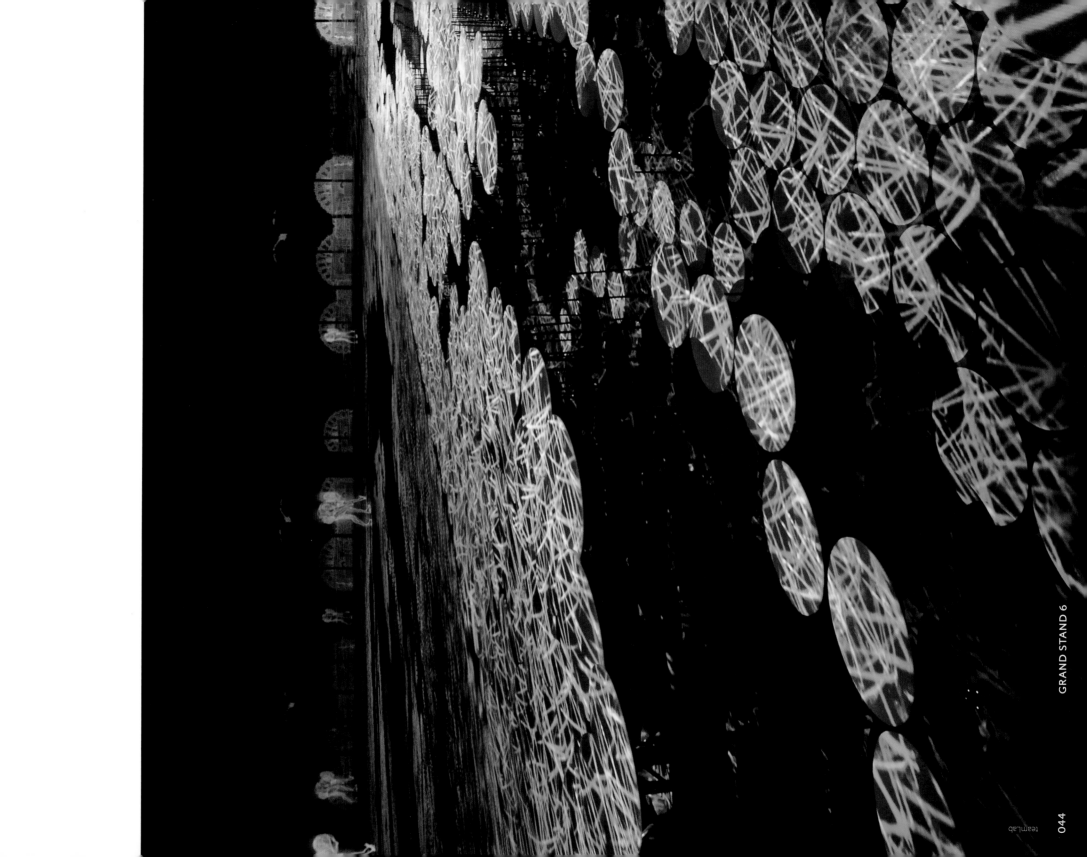

TEAMLAB brings the sublime, terraced rice fields of Japan to the country's pavilion at Milan Expo 2015

MILAN — Rice fields are capable of growing at different elevations in the dynamic and multifaceted landscape of Japan, and so came to symbolise not only bodily nourishment but spiritual harmony between humans and nature in the national culture. The Japan Pavilion, produced by Dentsu, at Milan Expo 2015 looked to this aspect of the country's gastronomical roots for inspiration in one of its exhibits. The immersive, interactive digital installation by art collective teamLab constituted a surreal and abstract rendering of these iconic crops.

Hundreds of small, round screens rose from the floor facing up toward the ceiling. These surfaces were mounted on flexible stems to resemble stalks of rice, and stood at various heights to imitate the terraced topology of the rice fields. An animated projection onto the screens represented changes in nature characteristic of the Japanese landscape over an entire year, and was accompanied by a large LED screen covering the wall opposite the entrance, as well as an ambient nature soundscape.

Visitors could wade through these stalks up to their waists, with the projection changing in reaction to their movements. By cladding the back wall in mirrors and the lateral walls in layers of half mirrors and monitors which projected seasonal elements, the field appears to spread out infinitely, allowing the visitor to be transported into the sublime.

Mirrors make the rice field appear to spread out infinitely

Screens mounted directly on the floor defined a main path through the exhibition, yet visitors were encouraged to roam off the path into the fields.

KNOBLAUCH swaps its trade fair stand for a bus, offering an experience-driven retreat

DUSSELDORF — In an unprecedented move, Knoblauch opted against a traditional stand for its presence at EuroShop 2017. Instead, the German studio was parked outside. Under the hashtag #beatofretail, Knoblauch's concept offered a relaxed and secluded haven from the bustle of the trade fair halls and the extremes of the weather, emphasising the importance of experience over transaction.

The team converted a vintage bus into a cosy espresso lounge, dubbed the #beatcafe. The interior design set maritime pine surfaces against black felt, with both built-in and moveable custom furnishings. A chimney stove provided warmth and enhanced the homely atmosphere.

Chats between staff and visitors were intentionally informal and had little to do with business deals, creating a casual and authentic experience that took one's mind off the hectic fair environment outside.

Along the back side of the exterior, a chaotic collage of reclaimed black furniture protruded from the vehicle, evoking the image of a nomad's capriciously packed rucksack. This sculpture also hinted at the most remarkable quality of the concept. Unlike a conventional trade fair stand, the bus was not discarded after the fair was over, since its portability and flexibility allow it to be rented out for future events.

Jens Pfisterer

The interior's pine surfaces were laid out in polygonal tiles with a small projection extending onto the ceiling like a crack, adding a dynamic accent to the decor.

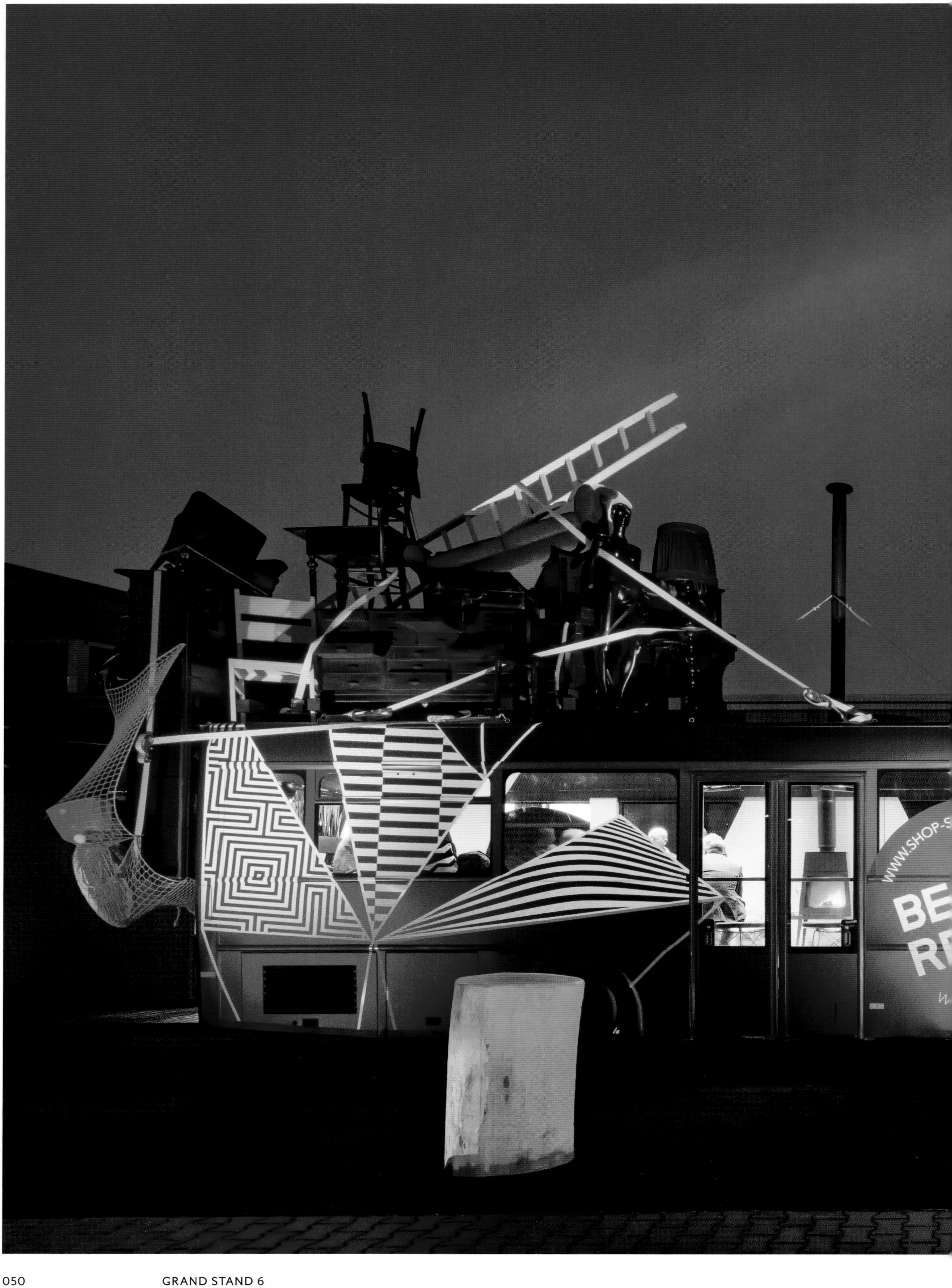
WWW.SHOP-S

A casual and authentic experience away from the hectic fair environment

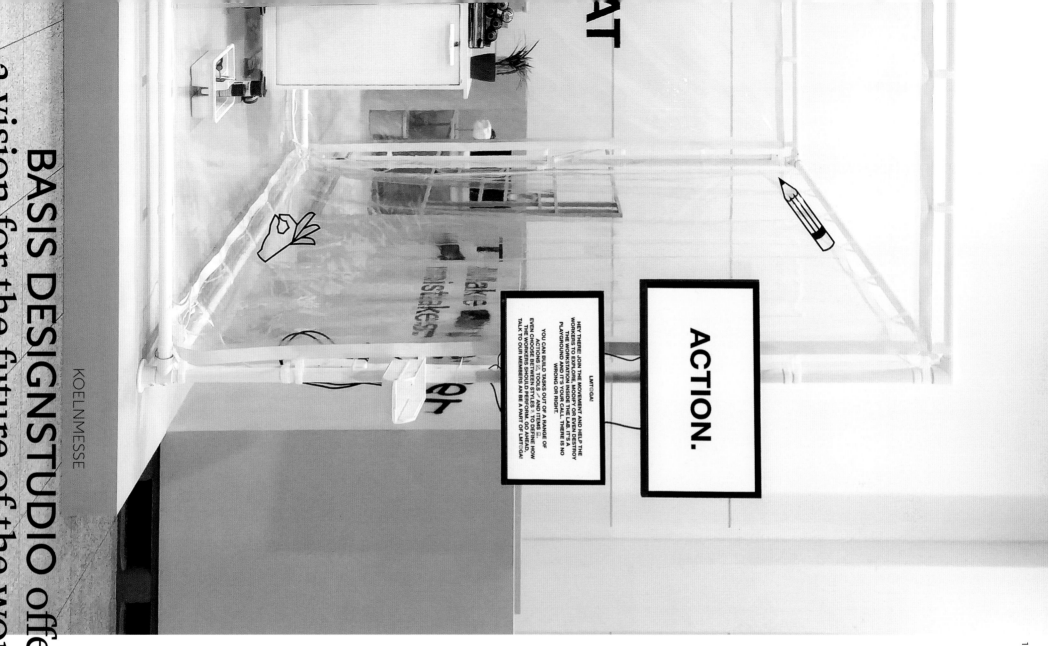

BASIS DESIGNSTUDIO offers

a vision for the future of the workplace through live creative destruction

ACTION.

LMT⊙GA!

HEY THERE! JOIN THE MOVEMENT AND HELP THE WORKERS TO EXPLORE, MODIFY OR EVEN DESTROY THE WORKSTATION INSIDE THE LAB. IT'S A PLAYGROUND AND IT'S YOUR CALL. THERE IS NO WRONG OR RIGHT.

YOU CAN BUILD TASKS OUT OF A RANGE OF ACTIONS ⟳, TOOLS ✐ AND ITEMS ⬚ EVEN CHOOSE BETWEEN STYLES ✂ TO DEFINE HOW THE WORKERS SHOULD PERFORM. GO AHEAD, TALK TO OUR MEMBERS AN BE A PART OF LMT⊙GA!

Than-Thao Tran

COLOGNE — Based in Dusseldorf, Felix Vorbeck and Johannes Winkler, co-founders of basis Designstudio, were invited to create an installation for Orgatec 2016. As part of a seminar at the city's University of Applied Sciences, supervised by professors Bernard Franken and Laurent Lacour, the experimental project was prompted by the question: How are people going to work and live in the future? The result was an interactive, performative installation that looked to 'show, that the development of a future-oriented and especially human workplace must be a collaborative process,' Vorbeck says.

In spite of its serious nature, this message was manifested in a playful, humorous manner. As Winkler puts it, 'our primary goal is that the fair visitors have fun through creative participation.' Borrowing from a well-known campaign slogan in the 2016 United States presidential elections, Let's Make the Office Great Again! was a laboratory comprising plastic foil stretched around a white scaffolding structure. Within this transparent tent, the designers staged a stereotypical office setting, where two mad scientists awaited instructions from visitors to alter its configuration.

Fair goers used tablets to combine terms from four categories — Action, Tool, Item and Style. These word combinations resulted in instructions which the laboratory workers would then interpret and act upon. While the experiment ended in a chaotic, nonfunctional mess, the booth encouraged visitors to value the creative process itself, full of trial and error, as well as its collaborative opportunities more than the end result.

1 The staged workplace featured notable furniture designs by Vitra, Lindemann, Hund and WINI.

2 Wearing suits that read 'Trial' and 'Error', the laboratory workers embodied the cycle of the creative process.

GRAND STAND 6

STUDIO BACHMANNKERN sets future against past to showcase a multifaceted line of lighting products

1 Semi-transparent curtains delineated the stand, at once functioning as a convincing home accent and allowing the lighting effects to be as visible as possible from the outside.

2 Visitors could control Ledvance's smart lamps from mobile devices, thus generating unique atmospheres.

Past stands back to back against future, their polarity accentuated by a striking contrast between light and dark

BERLIN — German lighting company Ledvance made its independent debut at the 2016 IFA after being sold by parent firm Osram. The brand commissioned Studio Bachmannkern to design a stand that would promote its dual specialty in traditional lighting design and modern LED technology.

To answer to this challenge of combining two contrasting product worlds, 'the idea of an interplay of light and shadow was born,' the architects explain. A large wall divided the exhibit's rectangular platform diagonally into two zones. Past stood back to back against future in a Janus-like configuration, their polarity accentuated by a spotlight cast on the latter.

'Smart Home' was the theme chosen for the white side of the stand, which represented the brand's technical progress. A geometric shelving system featured compartments that depicted the versatility of Ledvance's latest technologies by applying them to different functions and settings. Orange accents and objects completed the vibrant, futurist side and referenced the brand's logo colour. Meanwhile, on the opposite side, a rugged, retro design was chosen to present the Edition 1906 collection. Installed among exposed bricks and steel beams, the line's classic forms were presented as a possible illumination for urban loft architecture.

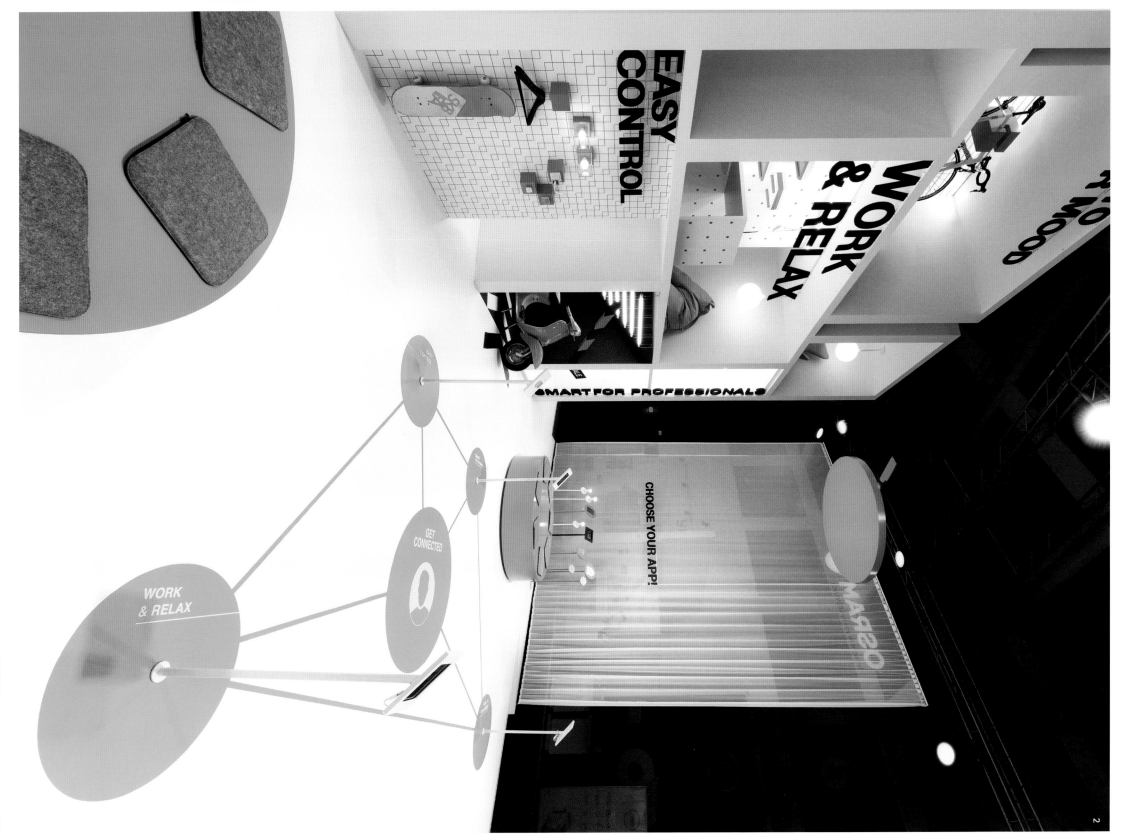

The cube installation consisted of 840 LEDplates fixed in groups of ten on 84 columns that were controlled by 14 motors.

Eduardo Biermann

GTM CENOGRAFIA
helps sportwear
brand celebrate the
unlimited potential
of everyday athletes in
an engaging space

RIO DE JANEIRO — With the help of São Paulo scenic designer and constructor GTM Cenografia, Nike brought its Unlimited campaign to the 2016 Rio Olympics. Intended to celebrate the stories and achievements of everyday athletes around the world and across all forms of activity, the brand narrative inspired both locals and foreigners to engage with the company's products and services.

The square footprint of the pavilion comprised two parallel exhibition corridors flanking a wide, outdoor walkway. Inspired by sea containers, the enclosed volumes took a rectilinear form and were clad in corrugated metal. At either end, the metal was cut away to reveal translucent polycarbonate plates, admitting natural light during the day and glowing from within at night. A colourful tunnel in one of the volumes displayed Nike's latest tennis shoes and led to an area where visitors had the opportunity to wear the same NikeLab Team Brazil Jacket worn by the country's athletes at the medal podium. The second space, mostly white, promoted additional products and featured a t-shirt customization station.

Above the walkway, bridging these two volumes, was a vibrant cube installation by Brazilian artist Muti Randolph. The dynamic, modular structure consisted of numerous moveable LED plates that created a three-dimensional projection of highlight moments from the competitions.

Visitors were encouraged to document their experience visiting the pavilion and wearing the jacket of the Brazilian athletes on social media.

SUPERB SOFTNESS

PRESSURE-MAPPED OUTSOLE PROVIDES TARGETED CUSHIONING

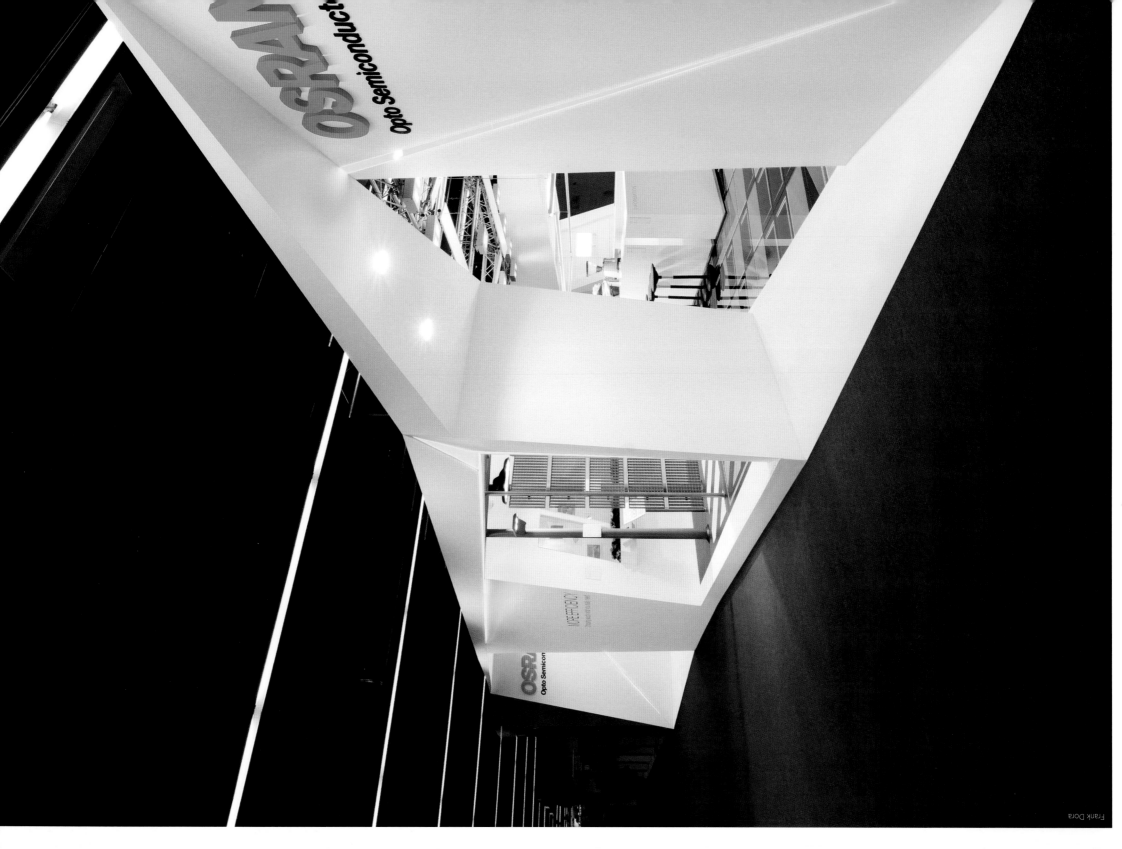

OSRAM OS

STUDIO BACHMANNKERN
gives a geometric, expressionist effect to LED technology

FRANKFURT – Bachmannkern's lauded collaboration with Osram OS attained new heights of lively experimentation at the 2016 Light + Building. The company's latest portfolio included a revolutionary new technology in LED chip sorting and thus required an equally ambitious and innovative display.

An imposing rectangular mass encapsulated the compact exhibition space. Guided by the theme 'from a sharp angle into a wide space', jagged recesses cut into the sides of the main volume formed intriguing entrances and explosive veins of orange light. Inside, visitors encountered three integrated sections, each devoted to key phrases in the brand's message: more efficiency, more quality, more flexibility. Each area provided ample space and seating areas

for dialogue and contemplation, while a large bar defined the centre of the floor plan.

Adding a vibrant, interactive aspect to the exhibit, an installation comprising a pressure-sensitive LED floor featured graphics that were triggered by the visitors' contact. To showcase the new product – TEN° binning – an irregular assortment of circular discs stood at one entrance in contrast to the booth's predominant rectangular forms. The sculpture demonstrated the sharpening of colour discernment possible with the groundbreaking mechanism.

A Competence Centre grounded the spectacle in a practical outline of the company's portfolio and helped visitors determine which product would best suit their needs.

The palette of materials, tones, and geometric forms of the bar area gave the booth a science fiction quality, conveying a laboratory for radical ideas.

An installation comprising pressure-sensitive LED screens on the floor is triggered by visitors' contact

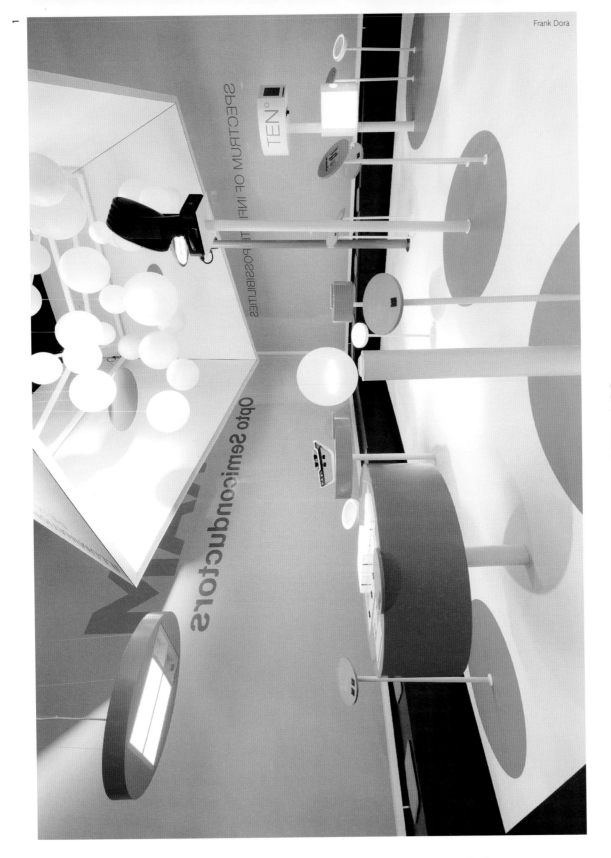

Frank Dora

1   In the Illumination exhibition space, a number
   of applications of Osram OS solutions were
   presented, including headlights, street lamps
   and ceiling lights.

2   A spacious circular lounge in the middle of
   the stand allowed visitors to enter the brand's
   world through virtual reality experience.

OSRAM OS

STUDIO BACHMANNKERN
unravels the vast potential of
lighting in a spectral design

MUNICH – No stranger to Electronica nor to
the work of Studio Bachmannkern, in 2016
semiconductor and lighting brand Osram OS
commissioned the Solingen-based designers
to create their stand for the fifth consecutive
year. A 'spectrum of infinite possibilities,' as the
exterior slogan declared, lay behind the towering,
translucent border of the cubic space, where an
interactive display introduced visitors to the
brand's products.

Beginning with the idea that 'light comes
in straight lines,' a spectrometer served as
the formal inspiration for the layout of the
booth. From this, the designers derived three
exhibition spaces topped by light cones:
Illumination, Sensing, and Visualisation. Each
space represented a specific aspect of Osram's

Opto Semiconductors, so the displays were set
in a variety of light scenes and used different
technologies to promote interaction between
visitors and product.

Illumination featured suspended globes
with animations projected onto them to
demonstrate the full potential of light. In Sensing,
cylindrical bars with pulsating light demonstrated
the role of sensor technology, and Visualisation
reminded visitors that light is the foundation of
image with rectangular surfaces of varying sizes
forming a dynamic video screen.

While focusing on the quality of the visitor's
experience in terms of comfort and exchange
of information, the studio's bold design helped
assert the idea that there is more to light than
meets the eye.

GRAND STAND 6

068

SPECTRUM OF INFINITE POSSIBILITIES

SENSING

ILLUMINATION

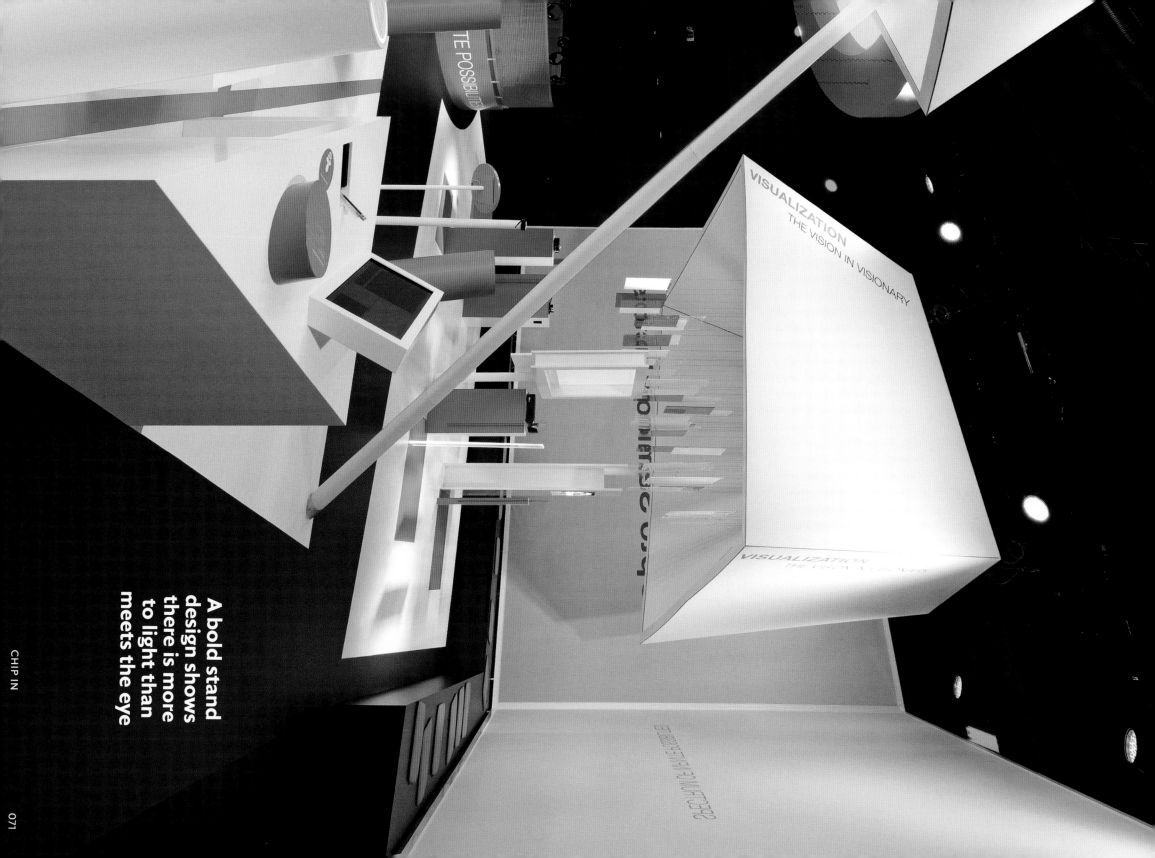

A bold stand
design shows
there is more
to light than
meets the eye

VISUALIZATION
THE VISION IN VISIONARY

PETER SCHMIDT GROUP
conveys the power of multi-sensory experience in retail spaces

1   Despite the compact floor plan and prominent popcorn cannon, the stand provided a cosy niche for social interaction and reflection, with timber boxes of various sizes stacked against the wall.

2   As the spatial design focused on the immediate, visual impact of the stand, information was provided through accompanying materials that further reflected the company's expertise in brand communication.

Retail environments can empower brands by curating multi-sensory experiences for consumers

DUSSELDORF — Having worked largely with brand spaces design, corporate and packaging design, and brand management and strategy, Peter Schmidt Group knows how to make a lasting impact with compact media. Sitting on a 15 m² footprint, the German company's debut at EuroShop 2017 embodied a clear philosophy: as an intermediary space between products and target groups, retail environments can empower brands by curating multi-sensory experiences for consumers.

Brazenly expressing this potential, 'We're smashing!' was the booth's leading catchphrase. An explosive design of clashing turquoise, black and yellow diagonal stripes cladded rectilinear

tiers of maritime pine, in a design aligned with the resurgent trend of the 1980s Memphis style.

The playful and conspicuous spectacle culminated in an abstract cannon, with its barrel serving as a functional popcorn maker. More than a simple gimmick or even a literal interpretation of 'smashing', this element represented the implementation of a multi-sensory experience in a retail space — with the sound of popping, the smell, and taste of the popcorn. Emphasising the importance of digital technology in the creation of this sensory experience, a wall wrapping around one side of the stand supported two angled screens framed into a circular display with synchronised animations.

Thomas Stefan

SEVENONE MEDIA

Visitors ascend into digital clouds at this marketing agency's stand by BENZ & ZIEGLER

The stand featured a variety of different seating arrangements that could accommodate a diverse range of activities, from intimate business meetings to conference talks.

COLOGNE — It's not often that the ceiling becomes the main attraction of a trade fair booth, if there is one at all. At DMEXCO 2016, however, it became the key player in creating an immersive experience for visitors at SevenOne Media's stand. Conceived by Benz & Ziegler, the Digitainment City presented a futuristic landscape of accelerated growth and connectivity that the German media agency strives to make possible.

A massive, amorphous fixture loomed over the exhibition space, with LED screens projecting a video of SevenOne's work to the stand below. Two recesses at its centre lent the ceiling the illusion of weightlessness and permeability. Suggesting the idea of a 'content cloud', its phantasmagorical ambience symbolised the dynamism of the expanding company and its motto: 'we are moving brands.'.

Beneath the cloud, the booth's interior elements appeared to rise seamlessly and organically from the floor, resulting in an integrative design that created the effect of a 'floating room sculpture'. A red pathway set against a white backdrop functioned both as an intuitive spatial orientation for visitors and as a link to the company's branding. At the centre of the stand, a grand staircase embodied upward movement, an ascension into the transient, rarefied stream of the cloud.

GRAND STAND 6

The booth's interior elements form an integrative design that suggests a 'floating room sculpture'

SCHMIDHUBER and **BLACKSPACE** create an all-encompassing experience of the connected home

Jörg Hempel

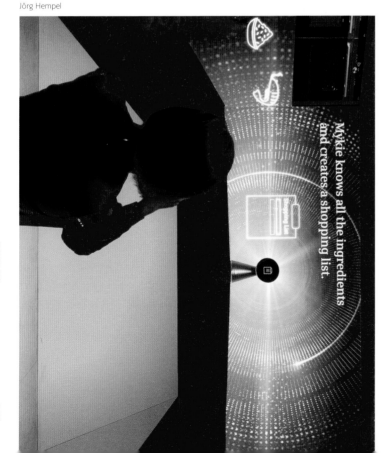

Mykie knows all the ingredients and creates a shopping list.

BERLIN – Siemens Home Appliances recognised that for its exhibition at IFA 2016, its products would have to be made tangible to the consumer, not relying simply on feature presentation. Their Urban Loft concept, created by Schmidhuber and Blackspace, implemented an inviting and all-encompassing experience 'of the real world, with all its "exciting possibilities", in the here and now,' the designers say.

A silver, polygonal volume housed the Urban Loft concept, with long, sharp recesses forming entrances and creating an open and diverse atmosphere in which cutting-edge, new products were presented in dialogue with high-end living environments. Vibrant, multimedia settings were created in order to demonstrate how the company's high tech solutions are able to not simply satisfy human needs, but 'elevate them to a whole new level.'

The centrepiece of the exhibit, reflecting a perceived trend of the kitchen as the centre of the home, was a cooking arena that showcased the company's 'Home Connect' solutions and offered a future of fully connected culinary experiences. Celebrity chefs utilised intelligent appliances such as Mykie, a personal assistant and command centre for the kitchen, and cookConnect, a cooking surface with an integrated extractor hood, in a cooking show that helped bring visitors closer to the brand's new solutions.

Siemens Waschmaschinen mit Home Connect.

Vibrant, multimedia settings demonstrate the company's high tech solutions

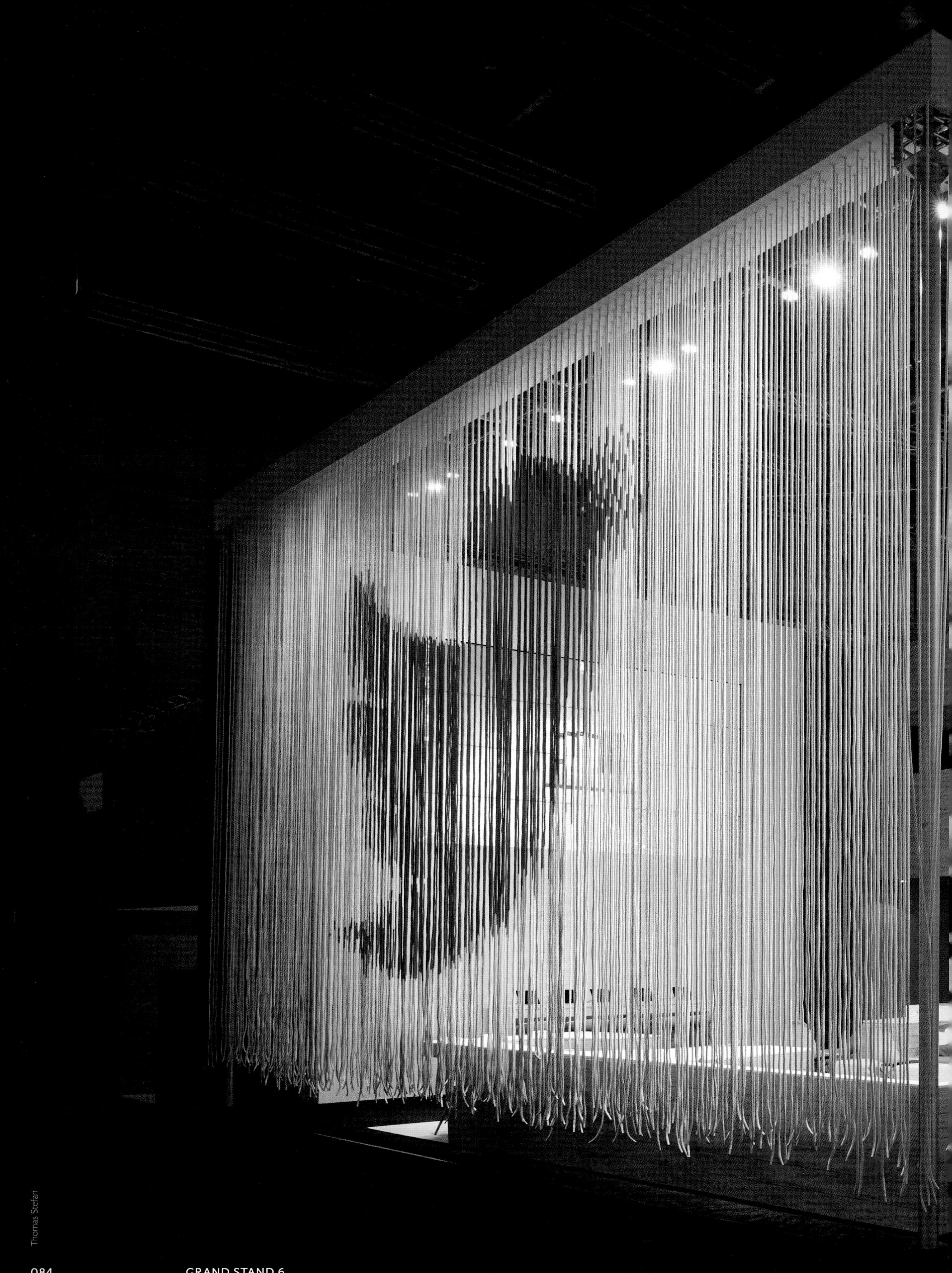

Thomas Stefan

BENZ & ZIEGLER
turns the immaterial
world of tweets into an
organic stand design

COLOGNE — Beyond simply being a digital service, the rapid, ephemeral flux and imperative brevity of Twitter's interface naturally evades any tangible identity. For their presence at DMEXCO 2016, Munich-based architects Benz and Ziegler attempted to translate the social media company's abstract product into a human, organic, physical presence.

Taking inspiration from the homogeneous format and structure of the microblogging unit, the studio created a 'forest of tweets'.

A layer of hemp ropes, embodying strands of communication, was suspended from a prefabricated steel frame to form a curtain that delineated the two-story space of the exhibit. The curtain featured a sprayed-on logo that became clearer from a distance, making the booth unmistakably conspicuous from all vantage points.

Entering these 'woods' symbolised a transition from public space to an individual Twitter space, through a barrier that was

neither entirely closed nor open, but flexible and transparent. The interior consisted of an understated, rustic arrangement of intimate, booth-style seating, flanked by a low-profile bar and information desk. Blue and white cushions invoking the brand's colours, along with pillows sporting hashtags, (at) symbols, and Twitter's logo, rested on angular wood fixtures. These design solutions contributed to a natural, minimalist serenity that reflected the simplicity and immediacy of a tweet.

1

The design translates an abstract product into a human, organic, physical presence

2

1   A Blue Room featured a 360-degree camera, offering interactive experiences for visitors and extending the 'forest of tweets' motif.

2   The delicate, flexible nature of the stand's envelop of communication strands made tangible the idea that people shape the world of Twitter.

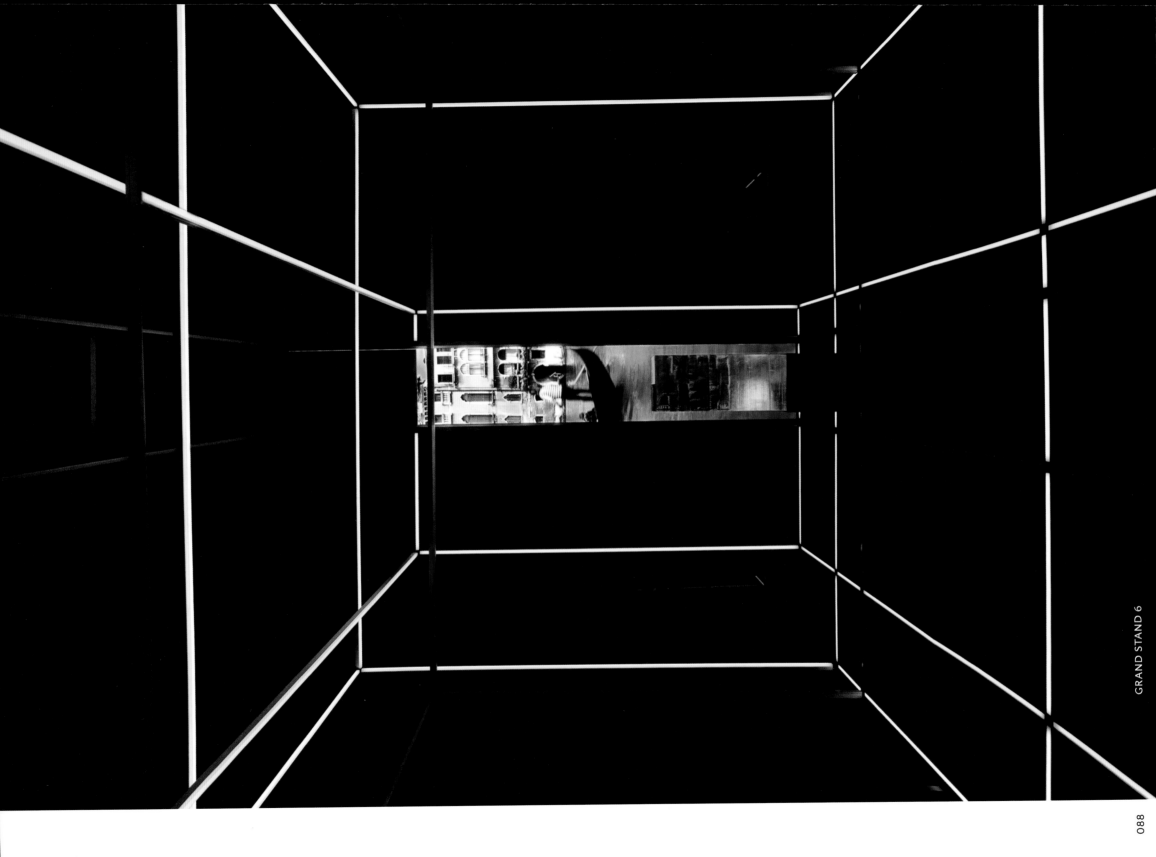

A multi-sensory installation by UEBERHOLZ depicts light as the catalyst of architectural space and perception

VENICE — Wuppertal-based designer Nico Ueberholz's work has frequently explored the concept of light as the creative force behind architectural space and phenomenological perception. His studio's installation at the International Architecture Exhibition of the 2016 Venice Biennale explored the radical limits of this theme, featuring a multi-sensory room that was to be experienced through lighting.

The 3 × 5 m anteroom appeared dark and lifeless upon first encounter, except for the sound of a slow heartbeat, as if in a deep slumber. Upon entering the room, visitors triggered contacts in the door and awakened its mechanisms. A network of white and orange

LED lights wrapped around the room alternately pulsated to reveal rectilinear spaces of varying dimensions and reflected softly against black anodized metallic surfaces.

Opposite the entrance, a narrow, virtual window depicting a view of the Grand Canal adapted to the expansions and contractions of space. A column in the centre of the room was crowned with gold leaf that shimmered in the animated lighting, establishing a three-dimensional connection between image and space. Its crest displayed contact and background information about Ueberholz, while a monitor on the left wall showcased previous works by the studio in the context of the exhibition theme.

Frank Dora

The colour scheme of the LED network established a tonal contrast between warm and cold.

Nico Ueberholz, Wuppf
Ueberholz GmbH
www.ueberholz.de

Mediatektur
Markus Busche, Balve
Busche Elektrotechnik

Typografie
Marc Muchowski und
Büro Longjialoux Gmb

VODAFONE

WHITEVOID connects major topics in the telecommunications industry with a dynamic light installation

HANNOVER – Vodafone tapped Berlin agency Whitevoid for its stand design at Cebit 2017, calling for an ambitious, interactive and multifaceted display that would represent the company's engagement with major topics currently facing the industry. Whitevoid developed the Giga Network concept, a complex and sprawling display portraying Vodafone as an innovative 'business enabler'.

The space was divided into four 'worlds' – Giga Netz, Giga City, Giga Retail and Giga Factory – each presenting clients whose business had been optimised by Vodafone in its respective context. The main attraction, an installation comprising 360 light fixtures with individually-controllable pixels spanned the entire exhibit and connected its diverse elements in a vast network.

Meant to convey data moving at the speed of light, these animated lighting patterns were synchronised with five large LED walls streaming video content. Another prominent feature of the booth was a physical model of a city onto which an animated, gesture-controlled information layer was superimposed when visitors wore AR headsets.

The theme of connectivity in daily life extended to an outside area, where visitors could experience services powered by the company's technology in real time. Overall, the stand's muted colour and material palette created both a professional business environment and a neutral backdrop for the technological features of the exhibition.

In Giga City, Microsoft HoloLens seamlessly connected holograms with the real world and allowed visitors to interact with digital content through simple, intuitive gestures.

Automotive brand shines anew with sculptural and interactive stand design concept by BLACKSPACE

PARIS – 'Think New' was the phrase chosen by Volkswagen to introduce ID, its line of electric-powered, self-driving, avant-garde cars. The company commissioned Munich-based design studio Blackspace to translate these two words into a design concept for its booth at the 2016 Paris Motor Show. To do this, the designers took the brand's ideal of technological innovation beyond its products and into a holistic multimedia installation.

Forming the spine of the 60-m-long floor plan, a central sculpture comprised white tensioning straps interwoven around a steel frame. The serpentine structure formed a Think New Walk that guided visitors through the space and conveyed an architecture dissolving into digital connectivity. Twelve LED screens of varying sizes were scattered across a wall, forming the backdrop for the stand, both visually and thematically. The dynamic pictograms used cinematic language to communicate the brand's message and its relation to technology and sustainability. Contoured tiers of seating beneath the screens allowed visitors a space for reflection.

Virtual reality and touchpoint stations added hands-on and immersive qualities to the visitors' experience, while QR codes throughout the exhibit invited them to connect and explore the stand with their personal smart technology. Adding a human touch to the technology-driven presentation, staff 'mates' offered personal tours to visitors, helping them to actively engage with the 'Think New' theme.

Different stages represented the four pillars of Think
New: Automated Driving, Connected Community,
Smart Sustainability and Intuitive Usability.

Virtual reality,
touchpoint stations,
and QR codes
add hands-on and
immersive qualities
to the visitors'
experience

WANZL

ATELIER SEITZ designs
an all-encompassing
shopping gallery for the
display of retail fixtures

DUSSELDORF — For the world's largest manufacturer of shopping and travel carts, assuring consumers of the product's relevance in the digital age has increasingly become a top priority. Atelier Seitz took on this ethos while designing Wanzl's stand for EuroShop 2017. Sporting the motto 'solid as a rock', the display reified the brand's identity as a reliable and adaptive stronghold in an ever-changing, technology-driven market.

Crafted in the studio's workshops, the stand comprised a massive, black shell enclosing the exhibition space. Representing a solid, fortified harbour in the midst of the fair's chaotic rush, the shell served as a backdrop for a multitude of animated hashtags, among which #uptrade firmly stood out. By fully integrating the brand's main message — uptrade with Wanzl — into the booth, the designers were able to build on the company's identity.

In contrast with the black shell, the bright, 1400 m² interior took cues from contemporary shopping malls and airport terminals. Recesses in either longitudinal side of the shell hosted concept stores, showrooms and museum shops that reflected Wanzl's store construction expertise. A central promenade displayed highlight pieces from shopping carts and access controls, to high-quality seating and display cases. Incorporating smart technology, these products presented a future retail environment in which customers, retailers and shopping devices are all digitally connected.

1

2

1   Diagonal slits on the booth's shell paralleled the motion of the hashtag motif.

2   A variety of store settings within the booth, including a candy boutique, a workwear shop and a think factory, showcased the breadth of possible applications for Wanzl's retail equipment.

POINT

OUT

Building narratives
through spatial design

GUIDO MAMCZUR, Managing Director of D'art Design Gruppe, reflects on the firm's long-time experience in the world of trade fairs and the construction of effective brand narratives through spatial design.

'By focusing on narrative, a brand becomes tangible and fun to explore'

The first *Grand Stand* was published in 2003. How has stand design changed over the past 14 years?
Trade fairs define the cutting edge of what is possible in terms of brand experience. Today we are moving closer to a seamless alliance between digital and analogue. If you compare recent stands to projects 14 years ago, we can see that media-technology has evolved from bombastic sensationalism to much more reasonable and useful contributions to brand experience. To put it briefly, 'digitisation' has a huge influence on society and therefore on what we do as designers. People, brands and their messages are changing constantly and we are gladly taking an active part in this development.

How can these fleeting spaces make a lasting impact on a brand's image? Temporary spaces are free from the shackles of permanent buildings, they can be much more experimental, focused and provide a preview of future developments. In this respect, they are an ideal solution through which to put new strategies or concepts to the test. It's like learning under realistic conditions. With the input you can improve the concept and turn it into something more permanent.

Engagement and interaction are necessary components of stands, but the focus on creating an experience through which visitors can actively engage with a product, concept, or company have become more and more prevalent. Do you think this trend creates a competitive precedent that will turn it into a requirement across the industry? How can space and design-focused stands compete? We do not see experience and architecture or design-driven as contradictions or competitors. Interaction aims to create dialogue and empathy, whereas a spatial-focus often leads to a more contemplative exhibit. Both should be seen as different, but equally valuable, ways of addressing people.

Large spatial volume, striking materials or impressive media installations are actually quite often found at the top of communication hierarchies, accentuated by interactive subsections. We think that the challenge rather lies in the smart combination of these two dimensions. It is imperative to create a seamless, fluent and meaningful communication between the two.

In *Grand Stand*, the text introducing Dart's projects mentions that, for the studio, 'communication is the most important starting point, while the design itself is the instrument to reach a solution' (Frame, 2003: p 74). Could you expand on this idea? The starting point is always the conceptual engagement with the brand or company and the people behind it. It is a search for the story worth telling or, if you are working for a longstanding partner, the meaningful and sensible continuation and development of what happened before — the next chapter, so to speak.

Open communication and direct engagement at a very early stage and between all the stakeholders are the ideal foundation for any project. This way, we start to find the right balance among the various wishes, goals and viewpoints, and to identify a strong, individual narrative. This can take the shape of a dream-like state of abstract perfection, a broken urban narrative, or a collaborative workplace layout. No matter the resulting design, the story guides us through it.

How do you approach a narrative through design?
Designing spaces becomes the implementation of the idea. Space is a language, and as with any language, you will find characters, syllables, old words and fancy new ones. Cast an eye over syntax, semiotics, protagonists and ideals worth fighting for and voilà, you get your own unique (brand) story.

What are the advantages of focusing on a particular narrative that drives the design? To put it simply, people are able to internalise and memorise stories best, that is basically how our brain works. What is more, some companies or brands offer highly complex products or services and a narrative is the most effective way of explaining their solutions. By focusing on a narrative, we enable an emotional approach to technological or complex topics for all users: a brand becomes tangible, sustainable and even fun to explore.

How do you balance the construction of fresh narratives for a particular fair or exhibition with a brand or product's own established narrative?
The fair design may be a step ahead of the other brand spaces or projects, but it is never detached from them completely.

You have to stay true to the brand, be authentic and consistent. We have always seen it as one of our main strengths that we do not seek to impose our look on a brand, but strive to stay true to its essence. We do not see that as a hindrance to the creation of fresh, modern and technologically up to date brand spaces and narratives, quite the opposite. You cannot arbitrarily alter an identity: brand trust is never gained by randomness.

Lukas Palik

DART leads visitors towards a gradual reveal of a luxury appliance brand's reinvented image

AEG

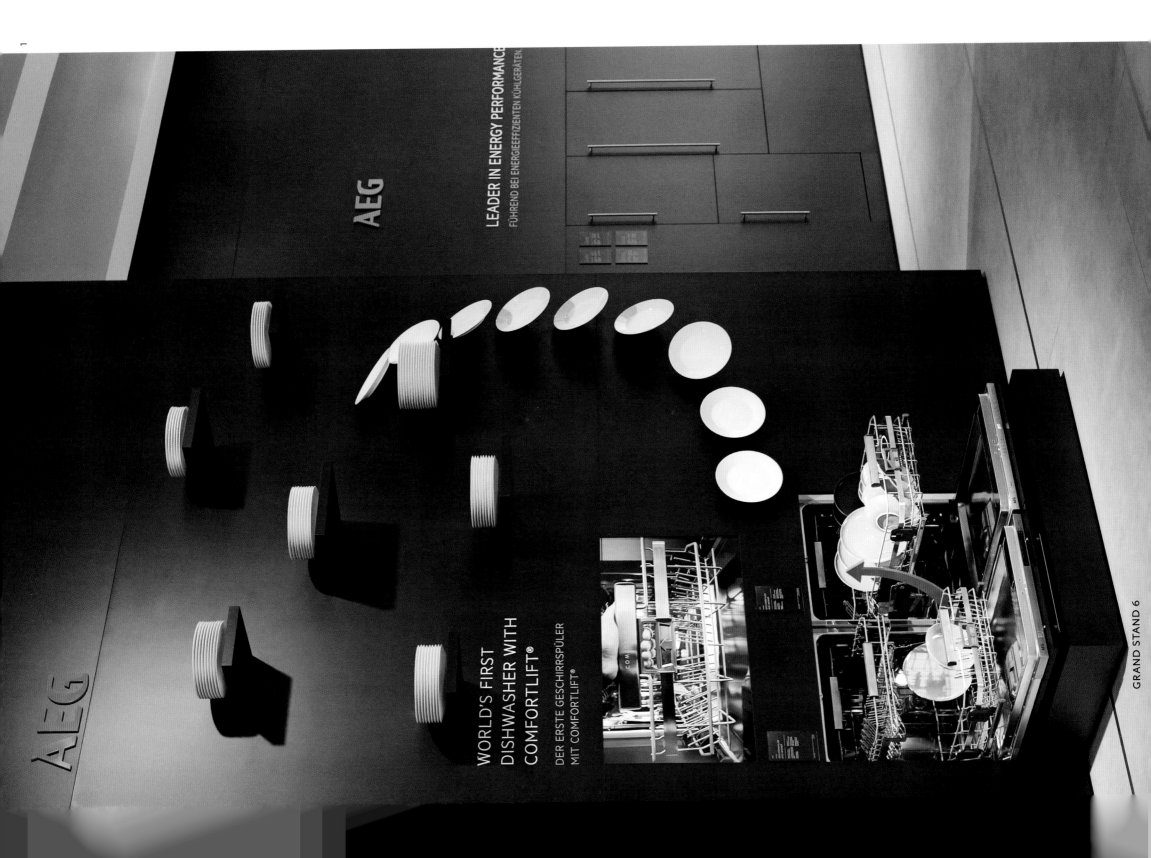

A sequence of walls creates a gradual reveal of the exhibition space

BERLIN — With two collections debuting to the public, Swedish appliance maker Electrolux felt its premium brand, AEG, needed not simply to show its new products, but an entirely new AEG image. German studio D'art Design Group fulfilled this request with its signature 'brand architecture' in an ambitious stand for IFA 2016, strategically realigning AEG's core traits into a cohesive and electrifying brand experience.

Using AEG's new logo and colour palette as the basis for the design, the booth evocatively welcomed visitors with the brand's three letters displayed against blue gradients each on its own floor-to-ceiling LED panel. Staggered at varying depths, these screens set the rhythm for

a sequence of grey walls that created a gradual reveal of the exhibition space. The predominance of elegant, dark hues was illuminated by bright light walls flanking both sides of the space.

Visitors entered to discover two product worlds for each new line: Taste, which promotes the Mastery range, and Care, promoting the Laundry range. Typographic and pictorial elements were juxtaposed with objects such as fresh produce and garments in eye-catching displays that reflected a modern and refined aesthetic identity, as well as an increased emphasis on implementing smart and ergonomic solutions.

1 Displays for products such as the Comfortlift used expressions of motion to illustrate innovative dishwasher racks that slide up ergonomically.

2 Highlight features of the appliances, such as a doneness knob on an oven, are magnified to create a playful, interactive experience.

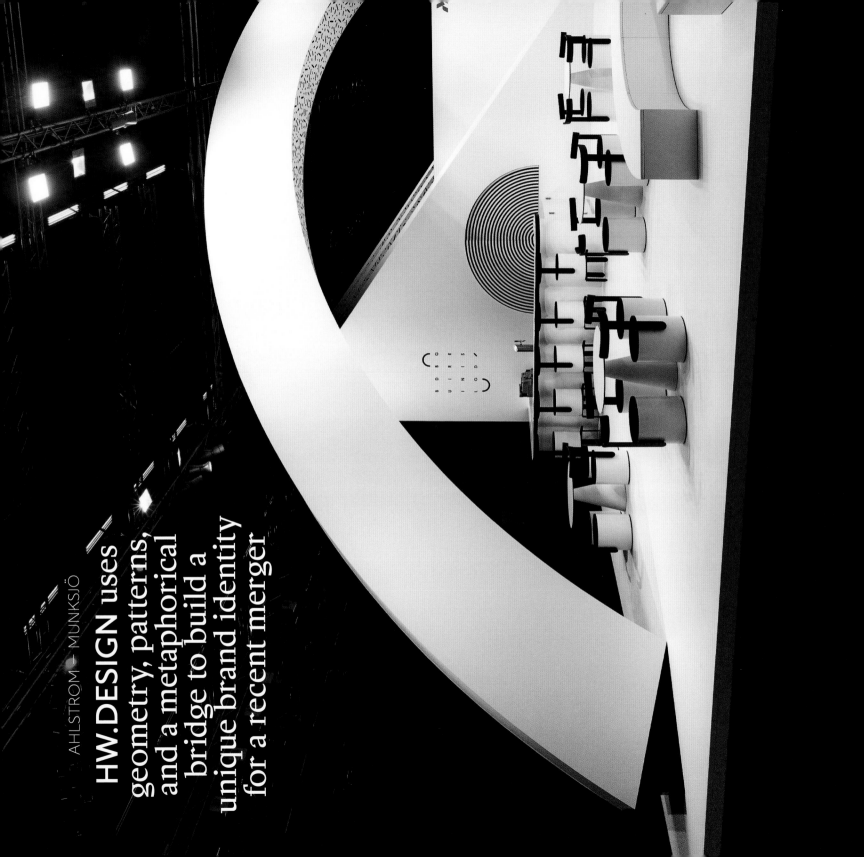

AHLSTROM — MUNKSJÖ

HW.DESIGN uses geometry, patterns, and a metaphorical bridge to build a unique brand identity for a recent merger

COLOGNE — Presented at Interzum 2017, the merger of specialty fiber-based materials and decorative paper firms Ahlstrom and Munksjö offered the opportunity for an ambitious and unique new brand identity. Taking 'Building Bridges' as its theme and the Memphis Group as its design inspiration, Munich-based studio hw.design combined bold forms with a minimalist, black-and-white colour scheme to affirm the values of the partnership and its impact on customers.

The stand featured a grand cantilevered arch that rose diagonally over the 220 m² floor plan, serving as a metaphorical bridge between the two brands, as well as between manufacturer and consumer. Basic geometric shapes formed the rest of the stand, like toy building blocks scattered on the glossy white, synthetic Decospan veneer floor. Covered in the same material, the sides of the triangular structures that flanked the stand served as the backdrop for the brand's new logo.

In a reinterpretation of the 1980s Italian design and architecture group Memphis, for whom decorative patterns played a major role, the studio introduced striking black motifs on the predominantly white surfaces. From a dot-and-dash pattern on the underside of the bridge to the radial op-art flanking the bar, they showcased the range of potential designs that can be achieved with the brand's products.

Serving as a platform for communication between brand and clients, the stand featured spacious meeting and lounge areas where geometric chairs and tables at once invited visitors to linger and served as a visual complement to the design.

Erik Chmil

The 'building bridges' theme stylised as a vision test was one of the subtle accents that beckoned visitors for a closer look.

Andreas Keller

AUDI

An ambitious pavilion by SCHMIDHUBER and MUTABOR highlights the powerful innovation of an automotive brand's latest models

FRANKFURT — Inspired by the release of its new A4 model, Audi introduced visitors of the 2015 International Motor Show to four main themes that made up 'the power of four' overarching concept. The grandiose exhibition, realised by Schmidhuber and Mutabor, comprised an emotive coordination of lighting, media, motion and sculpture that placed each of the company's new cars in a dynamic narrative that provided visitors with a tangible experience of the products' traits.

The spectacle was housed in a massive pavilion with sharp, angular recesses that defined an entrance on one side where the 'experience walk' began. Visitors ascended an escalator through a delicate, hexagonal framework that

grew organically from the facade. This structure represented the Audi Ultra theme, which capitalised on the lightweight construction, fuel efficiency, and alternative energy sources of Audi's vehicles. Next, a virtual window in the Audi Technologies area used AR to highlight the role of innovation in the company's output. The lifestyle and brand image of Audi Quattro could be discovered in a room carved out of ice that created plays of optical illusion and perspective. One was then finally hurtled through a rush of light and sound in the Audi Sport tunnel into the main hall, where the different concepts of the exhibition are come together.

A dynamic exhibition provides visitors with a tangible experience of the products' traits

1

1 The Audi Sport area re-created the sensations of a racetrack. LED lights on the ceiling conveyed motion and synchronised with a thunderous soundscape.

2 A rotating, oversized compass was placed directly above the new A4 model at the centre of the main hall, its needle pointing in turns to one of four large screens depicting each of the four key themes through a lighting, media and movement presentation.

3 In the Audi Technologies area, LED gaps on the ceiling, wall and floor symbolize data streams and digital integration in the automotive sector. In the back is a room carved out of ice.

BIRKENSTOCK

A vintage gym-inspired booth by **WALBERT-SCHMITZ** establishes a traditional brand into the field of sports at ISPO Munich

MUNICH – Almost 90 years prior, Birkenstock had invented the contoured insole that would revolutionise footwear forever, yet the famed German shoemaker was taking new strides into the sports market when it debuted at ISPO 2017. To generate brand awareness among these target groups while remaining committed to the company's high standards for production and materials, a booth by German studio Walbert-Schmitz transported ISPO visitors to an arena iconic of Birkenstock's timeless past.

The front of the rectangular exhibition space was styled after a vintage gymnasium, which was furnished with a paraphernalia of equipment from an old athletic facility in Belgium, including lockers, a bench and a

vaulting horse. This area featured integrated stations that assisted the visitor in finding the perfect Birkenstock for themselves. More importantly, the setting helped create a natural environment for the Birkenstock shoes, ideal for the sports world.

Like a Birkenstock shoe, every part of the booth was made from authentic and reliable materials – hardwood floor, wire mesh fence, and concrete covered walls. Behind the gym, a fitting room provided direct product experience, accompanied by services and activities such as foot massages. Shelves lining both sides of a meeting area showcased the entire product range and were flanked by LED screens and a bar.

Decorative elements like vintage jerseys and a punch bag further set the scene of the vintage gym.

DAIMLER

MUTABOR places a car maker ahead of its time with an exhibition space in the form of a clock dial

Ahead of Time.

HANNOVER — In the age of instant digital connectivity, time is more than ever the defining factor in a successful transportation and logistics system. German car maker Daimler unified its appeal to different target groups in the commercial vehicle market under this theme for its presence at IAA 2016 with the key phrase 'Ahead of time'.

Realised by Hamburg studio Mutabor in an area spanning two exhibition halls, the stand took the form of a large, elegant clock dial. The radial area created an open, continuous space for 65 vehicles and over 30 exhibits. The clock's hands, illustrated on the floor in large grey stripes, divided the plan into three product areas — vans, trucks and buses — and pointed toward two stages at 9-o'clock and 12-o'clock where presentations of success stories with the company's innovations took place.

Interactive exhibits featured live moderators in which the brand message could be extended into direct dialogue. Defining the 290-m-circumference, a ring of angled, moveable LED panels resembled a dynamic chronometer, bringing the time metaphor to life by constantly submerging visitors in new atmospheres.

Extra Wide

Extra Wide Flood

Light is the fourth dimension of retail

ERCO

Moritz Hillebrand

ERCO

ERCO declares the aesthetic sovereignty of lighting in retail design to promote its innovative, modular LED systems

DUSSELDORF — For German luminaire specialist Erco, retail lighting solutions are not simply a means of providing orientation in a shop or making the merchandise visible, but an aesthetic phenomenon in its own right that is essential to producing emotional responses in the consumer. At EuroShop 2017, the company showcased its innovative LED photometric and modular lighting systems that allow retail designers to implement diverse lighting parameters for projects of any scale or complexity.

The cubic stand was crowned by a hovering black, rectilinear volume that displayed the phrase, 'Light is the fourth dimension of retail.' Below this mass, amid contrasting white surfaces, a series of lighting scenes were set against an abstract wall design that silhouetted common shop display motifs, demonstrating the range of retail environments to which the company's systems can be applied.

Seven presentation tables offered visitors a closer look at the Erco's range of spotlights. Each table was illuminated by its respective spotlight, whose beams were modelled in a large, suspended sculpture made of yellow polymer. These elements offered visitors a unique perspective in conjuring possible applications of Erco's products, giving light a more tangible quality.

SIMPLE test drives a new corporate design for a retail solutions brand with a striking, symbolic stand

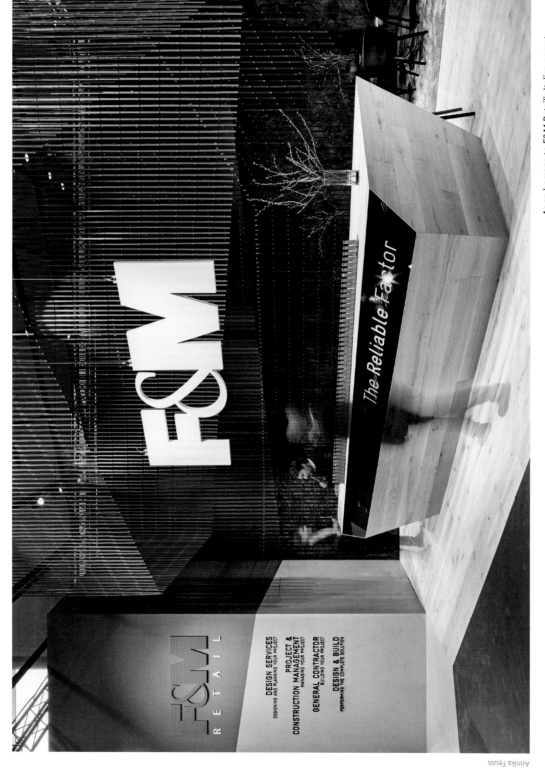

Annika Feuss

DUSSELDORF — Retail solutions agency F&M Retail commissioned Cologne-based studio Simple for an overhaul of its corporate design. With the tagline 'The Reliable Factor', the rebranding strategy emphasised the company's success in keeping pace with the everchanging retail environment and the importance of a trusted partner to realise retail interiors. The new image debuted at EuroShop 2017 through a tactile and memorable experience.

Though occupying a modest corner of one exhibition hall, the stand's presence was immediately conspicuous to visitors even from far away. A ceiling sculpture comprising of folding rulers formed both a chandelier and a curtain,

cast in the new corporate colours of red and grey. The ruler motif symbolised the transition of two-dimensional planning to three-dimensional reality. Light oak flooring, from which rose an angular counter, formed an inviting threshold.

Behind the curtain, uniform surfaces of grey carpet created an inviting corner. The three surfaces met seamlessly and continued the theme of concrete realisation, with the idea that it is when flat planes meet that they become a spatial reality. An interactive game involved visitors by challenging them to fold the rulers into specific shapes against the clock. This enlivened the social dynamic and engaged consumers directly with the brand and its services.

As an homage to F&M Retail's Italian parent company and its corporate colour, red Bitterino drinks were offered as a refreshment.

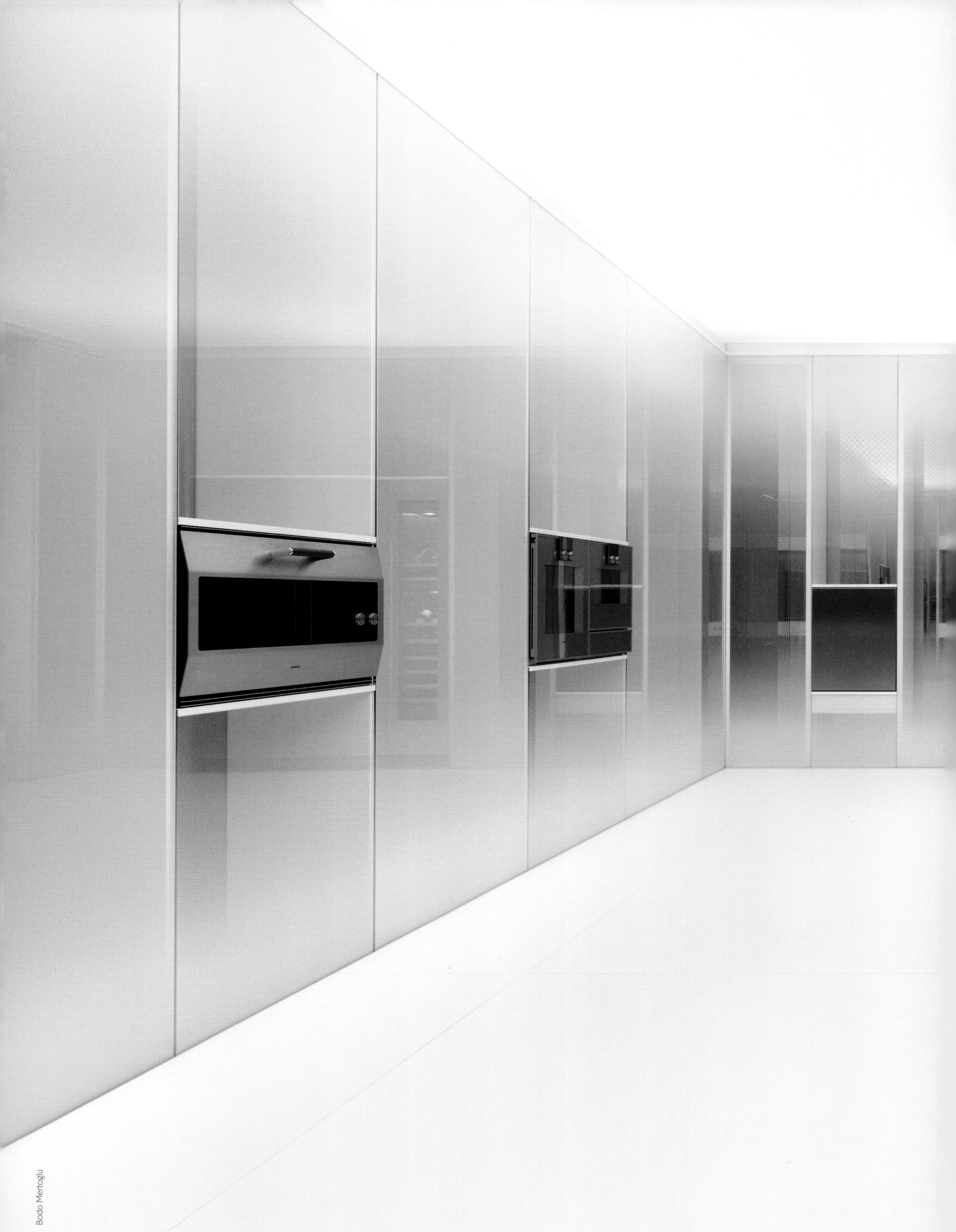

Bodo Mertoglu

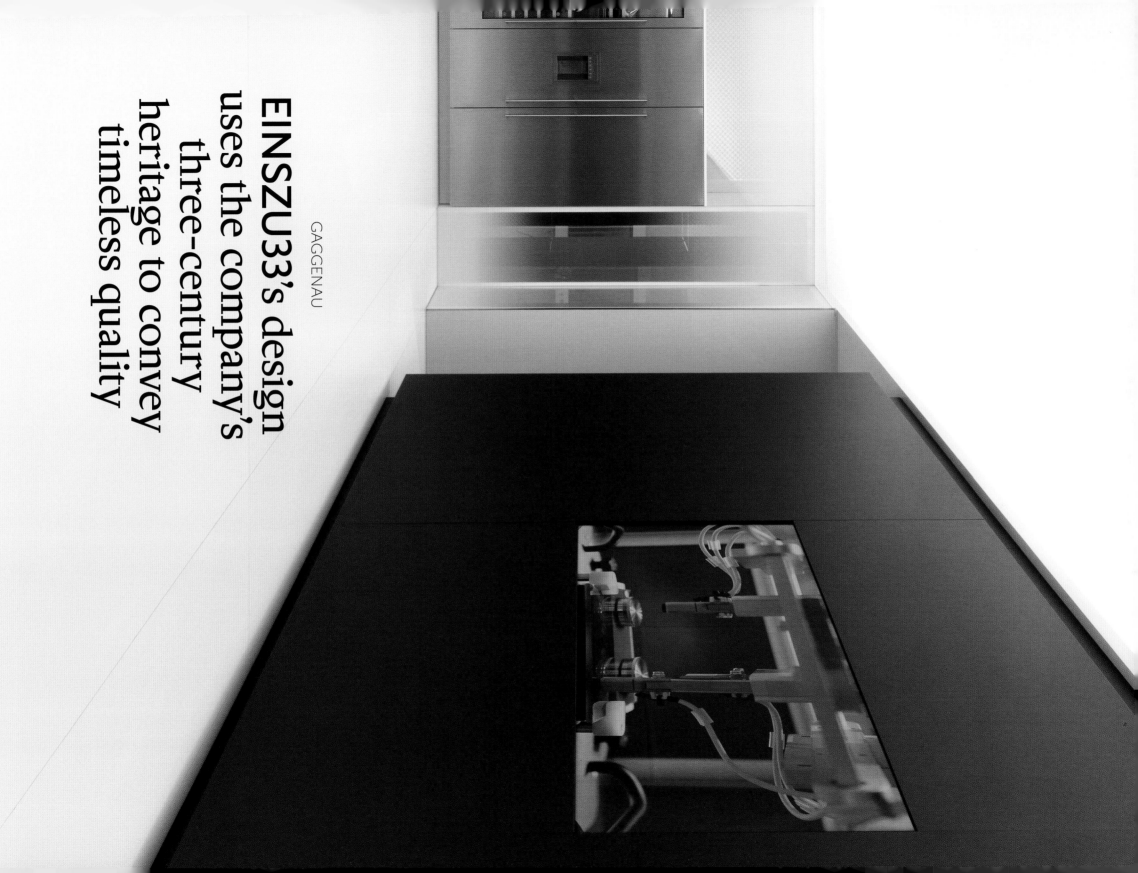

EINSZU33's design uses the company's three-century heritage to convey timeless quality

MILAN – As part of a campaign to celebrate its 333rd anniversary, German appliances company Gaggenau made an appearance at the 2016 Eurocucina. The booth, designed by frequent collaborator einszu33, guided visitors through the brand's history in the manner of a museum exhibit, curating a narrative of a timeless design philosophy defined by the oxymoron 'traditional avant-garde'.

A massive black cube defined the space of the booth, carved out with trapezoidal recesses to create enticing entryways and windows. Throughout the stand, as history unfolds, rustic Douglas fir floors finished with lye and soap give way to a white, lacquer flooring.

As with other Gaggenau installations worldwide, the booth incorporated its roots in ironworks through the presence of blacksmith imagery. An authentic representative of the industry gave live demonstrations of traditional methods that would have been used to forge Gaggenau's original products.

Informative texts and displays featuring artefacts historically associated with appliance manufacturing, further delineated the development of the company's modern production processes. These displays culminated in the 'room of perfection', a large glass cube that presented the company's latest product, the EB 333 oven. The double-layered wall of the cube allowed the presentation to appear like an exhibition piece from the outside, while on the inside the translucency gave the room the feeling of a distinct point in time and space from the other areas of the booth.

1 A timeline of major historical events made visitors aware of just how much world history the Gaggenau legacy has lived through.

2 As part of the exhibition, a representative of the industry gave live demonstrations of traditional manufacturing methods.

3 The star of Gaggenau's new portfolio, EB 333 stood apart from the other appliances in an understated and yet elegant black fixture.

The exhibition culminates in a large glass cube that presents the company's latest product

INSTA

An abstracted form of a power station by
UEBERHOLZ suggests permanence
and stability in lighting products

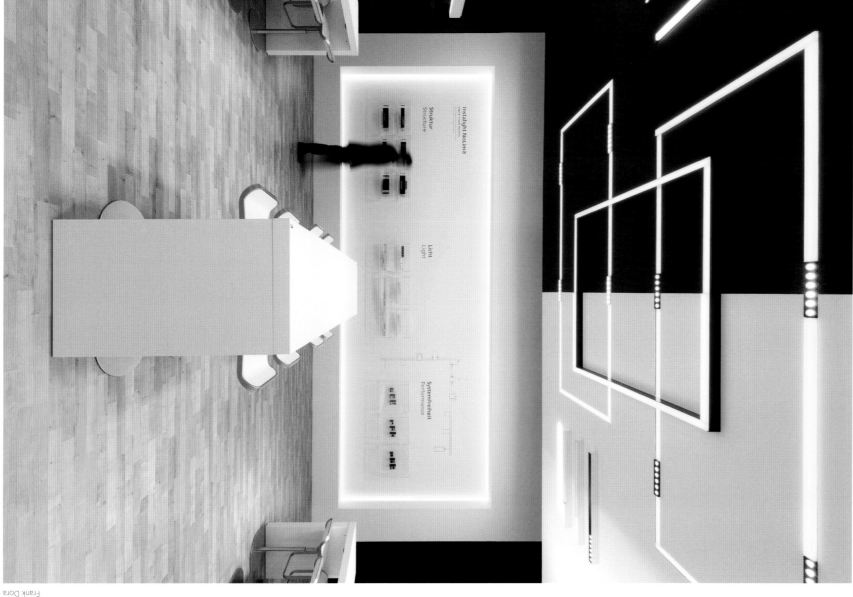

Frank Dora

FRANKFURT – To promote NoLimit, a new line of linear and modular lighting fixtures by German company Insta at Light + Building 2016, studio Ueberholz designed an abstract power station. The display presented the company as a reliable provider of lighting products and illustrated its specialty in building automation.

A series of tall, robust black facades defined a 10 × 23 m floor plan. The aggregate structure suggested permanence and stability and culminated in a monolithic, fibreboard portal with the brand's logo beaming weightlessly on the wall above. Inside, a wood-grain floor contrasted with black and white laminate surfaces on the walls and ceilings, at once connecting with the rustic quality of a typical power station and the bold futurism of the company as a technological powerhouse.

Breaks in the facades defined three distinct sections for the stand, including a central exhibition space and a hospitality area. Product display was designed like an art gallery, with light fixtures mounted on walls or suspended on the ceiling. Three long, standing tables at the centre of the display left room for conversation, so that this area served both as a showroom for Insta's latest wares, and a forum for discussions.

ISTITUTO LUCE-CINECITTÁ

An immersive, iridescent pavilion by NONE COLLECTIVE tells a story about Italian identity

1   Smaller LED screens suspended from chrome
    tube clamps appeared to float inside the 'crystal'.

2   The mirrored tiles on the floor were a solution
    to the need of visually enlarging the installation.

The crystal-like installation serves as a powerful allegory for the gesticulations that accompany Italian speech

CANNES — Each year, the Italian Pavilion coordinated by the Istituto Luce-Cinecittà at the Cannes Film Festival both promotes the country's cinema and highlights some aspect of the Italian identity. For the 2017 edition, Roman studio None Collective created an immersive multimedia installation titled The Brilliant Side of Us that explored the rich complexity of gesturing and expressiveness in Italian communication and its representation in cinema.

A parametric mesh made up of 704 wooden bars and 264 knots enclosed the 120 m² exhibition area. Its interior was coated in Mylar, a strong polyester film whose reflective and plastic components allowed the designers to create a jagged, but effervescent texture which intended to depict the centre of a crystal. Archival images of Italian movie stars manifesting typical gestures were played over nearly 50 m² of LED tiles, put together into screens of varying sizes. These fragmented faces, hands, and bodies were scattered throughout the room and visitors were invited to analyse each of them as isolated pieces before a final large screen recomposed them into a complete whole.

The crystal-like space was illuminated by a sound-reactive lighting system custom-made by Beam Light. Synchronisation between sound, light and the fragmented images, as well as a floor completely lined with mirror tiles, made for an other-worldly, immersive experience that served as a powerful allegory for the gesticulations that accompany Italian speech: though perhaps rough and unfamiliar upon a first look, they are a radiant, precious gem when illuminated.

POINT OUT

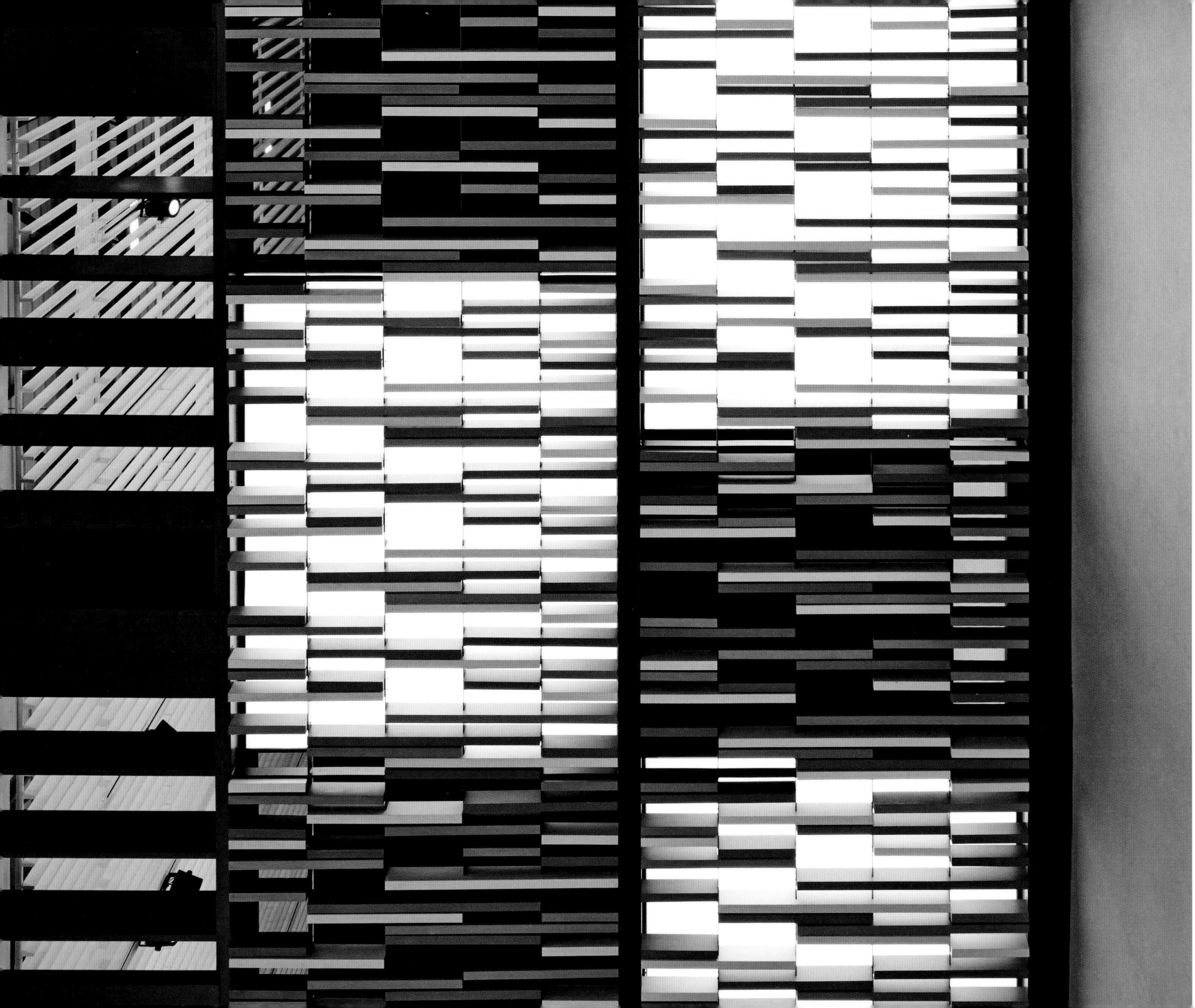

Luca Rotondo

KALE

PAOLO CESARETTI employs a unique geometric and chromatic vocabulary to showcase interior products

ISTANBUL – Unicera's hometown is a landscape coloured by contrasts, most conspicuously the tension between the archaic and contemporary. Paolo Cesaretti incorporated this aspect of Istanbul into his booth design for Turkish tiles, sanitary ware, faucets and bathroom complements conglomerate Kale at the 2016 edition of the fair, creating a distinctive and cohesive platform for the company's broad range of product collections.

Using simple materials and geometric shapes in innovative ways was part of a design strategy that looked to evoke the brand's main vocations: research, quality and style. Around the perimeter of the 750 m² exhibition area, vertically-oriented, patterned grey blocks were backlit through staggered LED light panels to form a semi-transparent, proto-digital 'tapestry'. The horizontal motion of this visually dynamic facade invited visitors into the space's open, homely interior.

Inside the largely open-plan space, various angled, semi-enclosed divisions were clad in intermittent plywood stripes, serving as display, meeting and administrative areas. The colour scheme was carefully chosen to connect symbolically with both professionals and consumers, with white embodying the company, different shades of grey delineating the brand's four product groups, and wooden tones evoking its commitment to sustainability. These chromatic and formal combinations managed to enhance the decorative and plastic qualities of the products while still clearly showcasing their technical specifications.

The main principle comprised a series of overlaid linear and monochromatic elements that, in tandem, formed unique perspectives from different angles and added a rich sense of depth to the space.

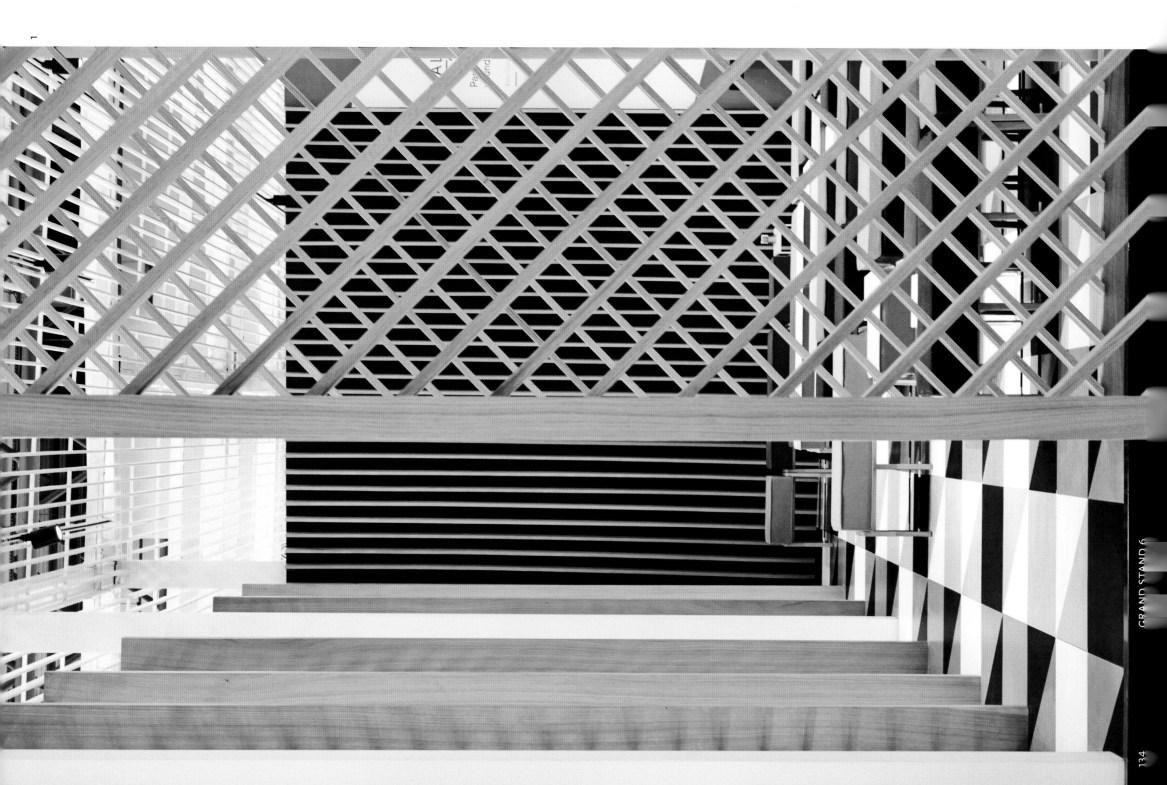

In the lounge area, the diagonal lines of the oak panels complement the motion of the ceramic tiles on the floor.

A chandelier-like installation of suspended white tubes suggested the flow of the faucets on display below.

A smart use of simple materials and geometric shapes evokes the brand's main vocations: research, quality and style

2

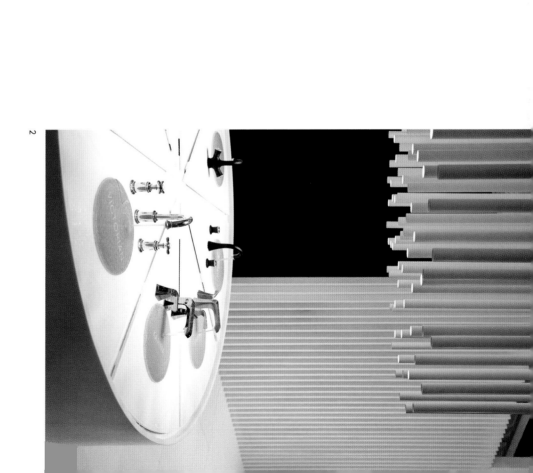

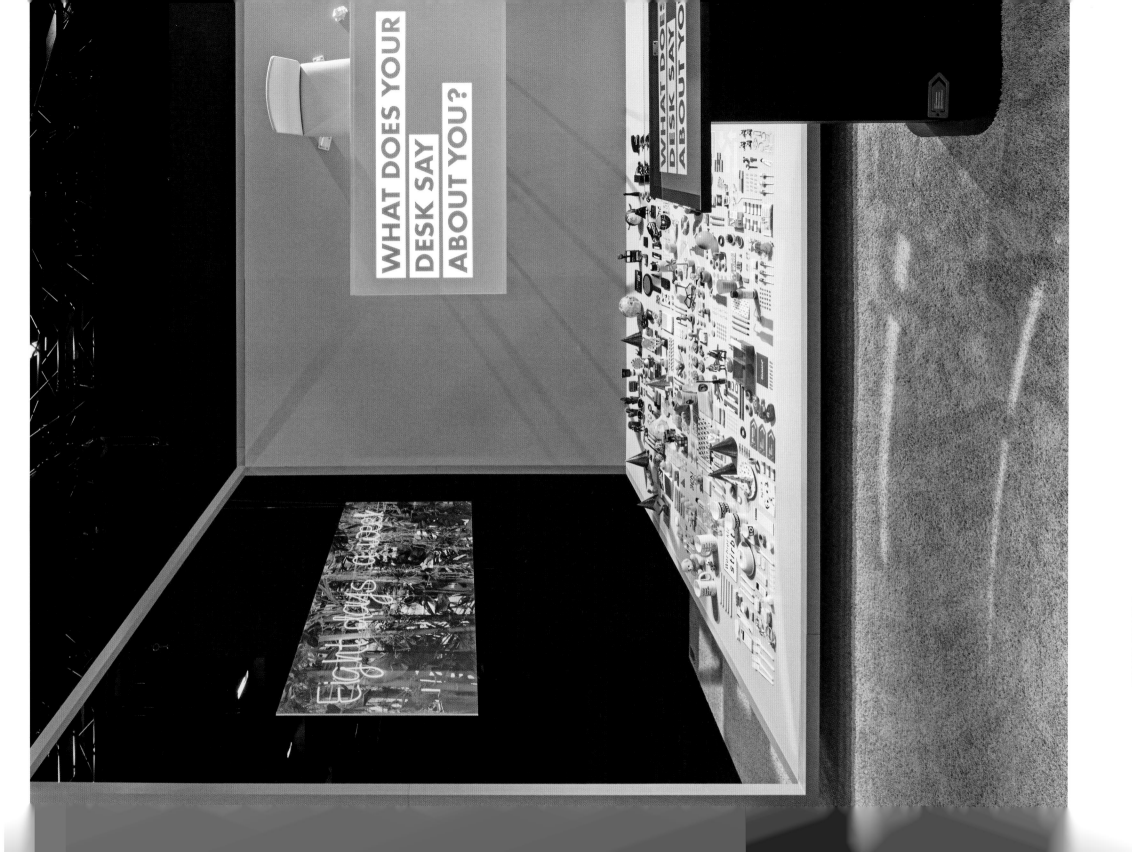

KOELNMESSE

An installation by IPPOLITO FLEITZ GROUP explores the relevance of traditional office archetypes today

Philip Kistner

COLOGNE – 'Does the office still make sense?' This question was the starting point for Ippolito Fleitz Group's Re/Work installation at Orgatec 2016. A sprawling exhibition with numerous high-profile collaborators, Re/Work examined the relevance of the traditional workplace in the face of the gig economy, a more transient workforce and digital networking technologies that allow employees and businesses to carry out tasks and meetings remotely.

The exhibition's resounding answer was that space remained a tangible counterpart to digital technologies and an inevitable conduit of identity. With this principle in mind, eleven spaces embodying office archetypes showcased the possibilities of their integration with the

changing nature of labour. The conference room was presented as an overlay of real and virtual. A wall bisecting a table horizontally featured video screens on each side projecting the other end, connecting distant interlocutors at eye level. Catering to the increasing need for constant stimulation, a table with an interactive touchscreen enlivened the waiting room experience. A tapered desk by Walter Knoll allowed members of a dialogue to define their relationship to each other, while a model by Pegasus integrated comfort and efficiency into a home office environment. Implementing one of Okinlab's freely configurable shelving systems, a library served as a secluded retreat.

Re/Work argues that space remains a tangible counterpart to digital technologies and an inevitable conduit of identity

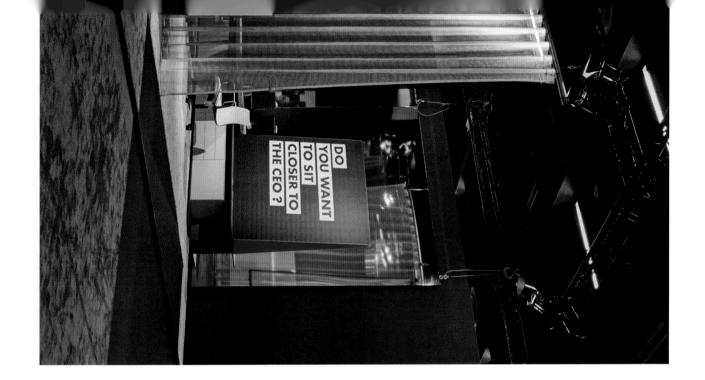

1   A meticulous and colourful collage of found
objects explored the personalisation of desks
as one's own.

2   Punching bags represented the sparring of
ideas and opinions through intense yet
constructive channels, fulfilled by digital
whiteboards behind that allowed for a
spontaneous flow of ideas.

2

DAS HAUS
2016
SEBASTIAN
HERKNER

SEBASTIAN HERKNER challenges conventional ideas of interior with a bold statement for 'barrier-free' living

KOELNMESSE

COLOGNE — Since 2012, IMM Cologne's Das Haus series has invited a special guest designer to create an installation for the fair that expresses their own ideal for a domestic living space. German designer Sebastian Herkner was chosen for the project in 2016. The radical subversion of his work went beyond simply the configuration, elements or atmosphere of an interior, challenging the very concept of interior itself in a bold, architectural gesture.

Rather than building a standard model apartment, Herkner constructed a circular, open-plan space with concentric layers of sliding curtains forming soft walls. Carefully-chosen fabrics of diverse colours and texture created a

unique, dynamic and at times collage-like tactile experience. The tiers of living area created by the curtains were connected seamlessly by a gallery, suggesting the idea of an 'endless house'. The core of the structure was open above, serving as an inner courtyard and a gathering point.

A semi-transparent cube containing the bedroom and bathroom extended out from the circle, offering privacy without compromising the openness of the residence. While evoking the classical Japanese pavilion, this 'barrier-free' living space carried a contemporary political message: a call for openness in the midst of Europe's growing right-wing isolationism.

The space carries a contemporary political message: a call for openness in the midst of right-wing isolationism

Herkner combined his own furniture designs with some of his favourite pieces by other designers, placing them around the space as if on a stage.

Curtains for Herkner's Das Haus installation were produced and sponsored by German textiles manufacturer Nya Nordiska.

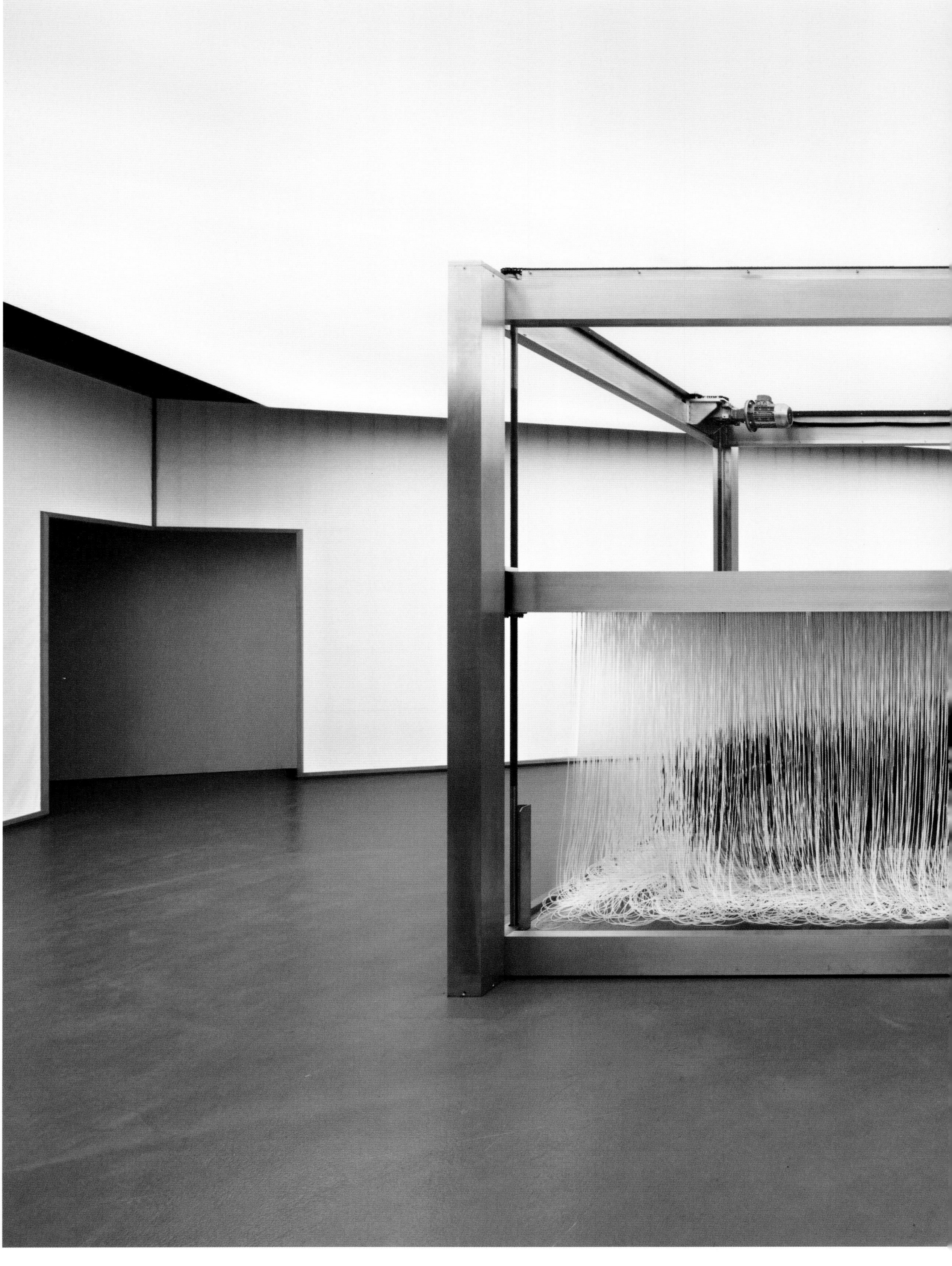

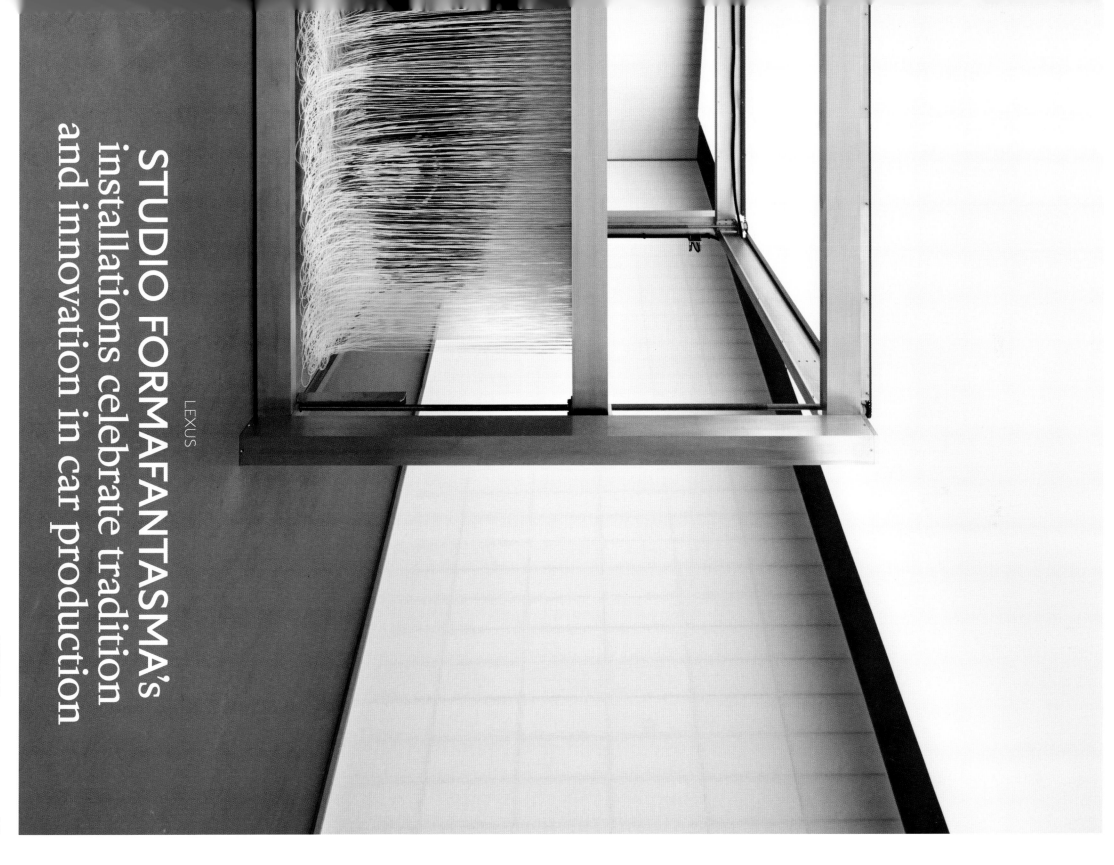

STUDIO FORMAFANTASMA's
installations celebrate tradition and innovation in car production

LEXUS

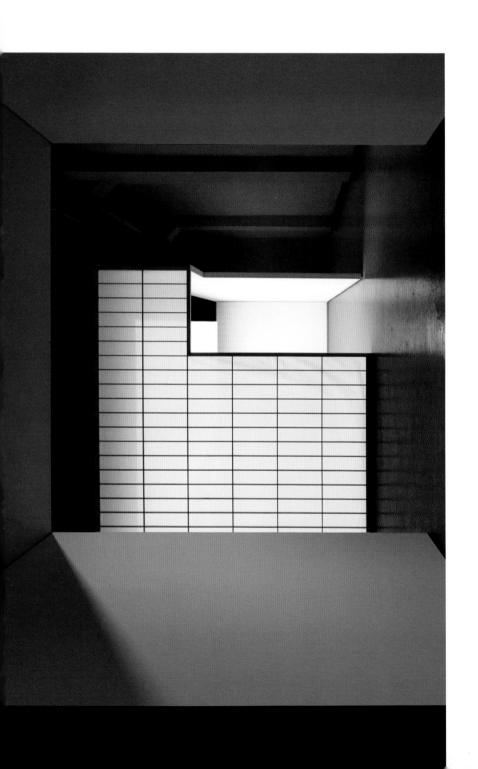

MILAN – For its presence at the 2016 Salone del Mobile, Lexus chose the theme of 'anticipation'. Studio Formafantasma interpreted this brief by identifying elements in the luxury car maker's production that would be essential to the future. Specifically, the increasing focus on ecological impact and the revival of craftsmanship and tradition. Occupying a former metal factory, three site-specific installations delineated these aspects of Lexus' vision within the context of the company's new LF-FC model.

The first space hosted a large kinetic light apparatus, comprising four stainless steel geometric sculptures with mounted LED tubes. The pieces rotated slowly to a subtle choreography over a smooth, reflective pink platform, powered from beneath by a mechanism similar to that used in the hydrogen fuel cell technology of the new model.

In contrast, the second room hosted a static and minimalistic exhibit. A series of black metal stools were arranged in a circle, creating a mystical and primitive Stonehenge-inspired atmosphere. The stools were finished with the same paint process used in the car's production. This method is derived from Japanese lacquering techniques and results in a complex tone that appears dark grey or blue, depending on the lighting. Exploring Lexus' roots further, a final installation featured a loom with thousands of threads that, when stretched, depicted the outline of the LF-FC. The piece served as an homage to Lexus' mother company, Toyota, which started as a textile company.

The interiors of the factory were illuminated by light boxes that referenced traditional Japanese architecture.

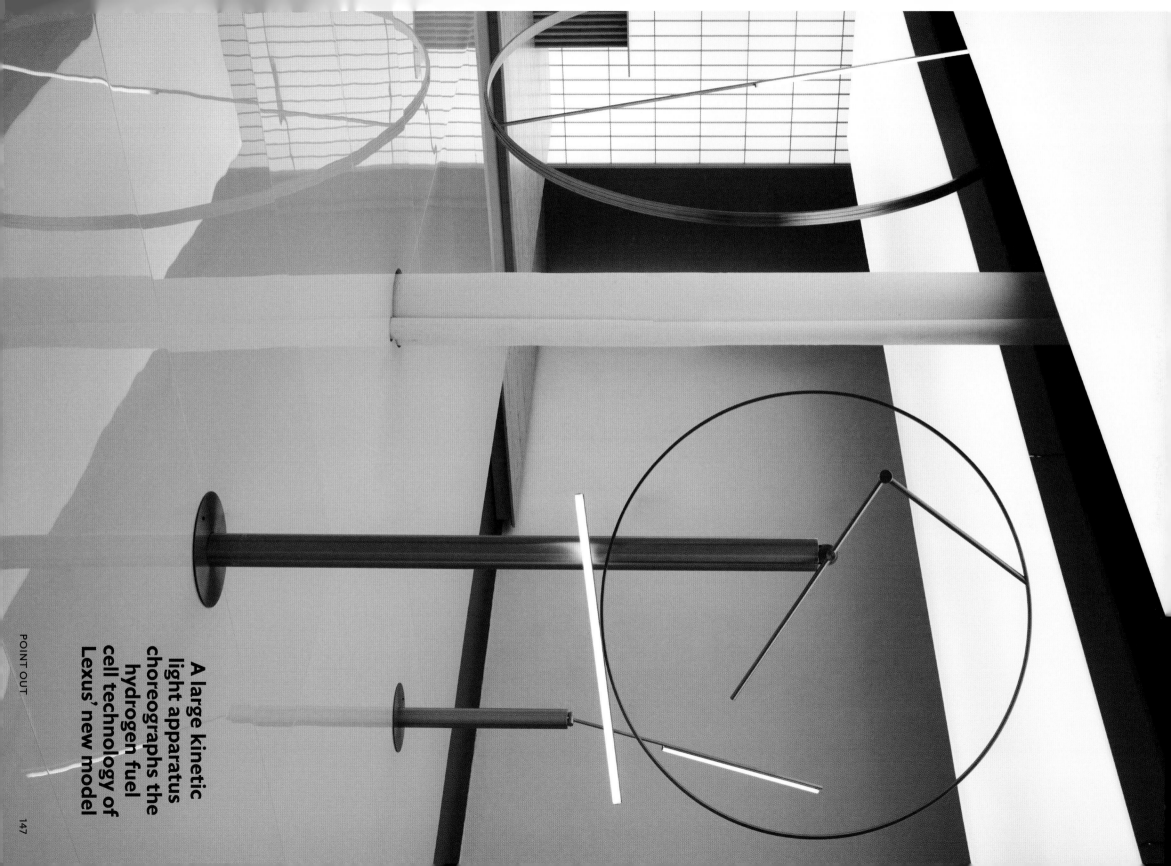

A large kinetic
light apparatus
choreographs the
hydrogen fuel
cell technology of
Lexus' new model

STEFANO COLLI
unifies a carpet brand's diverse collections with a strong and singular material language

MILAN — Over its 30-year-history, Nani Marquina became one of the premier brands in avant-garde carpet design. Its product offerings have grown from the designer's own works and commissions to market handmade pieces from India, Nepal, Morocco and Pakistan. For the company's presentation at Salone del Mobile 2016, the display required a common language, a discourse that would unify the diverse collections while not distracting from their individual qualities.

The concept, devised by Barcelona designer Stefano Colli, communicated the brand's values in a single material: wood. Pine boards covered the floors and walls, creating a warm and enclosed atmosphere that was inviting and conspicuous from the exterior. Highlight pieces displayed against these pine walls immediately conveyed the organic and refined craftsmanship of the company.

In the centre of the room, a striking orthogonal structure made from pine slats served as an organiser for the carpets. Its modular components allowed it to adapt to different spaces and products as needed. The lattice extended up from the floor to ceiling and was repeated across the roof, where it could support a variety of lighting elements. The interaction of light and form extended deeper with the complex geometry of shadow and reflection cast by the matrix.

Meritxell Arjalaguer

NEMO

STUDIO VALENTINA FOLLI sheds light on Le Corbusier and Charlotte Perriand

KORTRIJK – La Luce, an exhibition presented by lighting company Nemo and curated by Milan-based designer Valentina Folli in collaboration with her studio UNA.works, examined the works of Le Corbusier and Charlotte Perriand in the field of lighting design. Set for a multi-city tour, the display required not only portability, but also adaptability to different settings, while safely showcasing original prototypes and archival material.

One of the exhibit's stops, the 2016 Biennale Interieur in Kortrijk, proved particularly challenging for assembly because of its wide, cumbersome site, consisting of a terraced walkway flanked by two wheelchair ramps. Folli resolved this spatial complexity by dividing

Perriand's and Le Corbusier's works between the two ramps. The paths met at a central common area, where six coloured tables displayed common historical documents. To give continuity to the sprawling and fragmented space, Folli made predominant use of a light pink colour – chosen among Le Corbusier's architectural polychromy – throughout the exhibition.

For the exhibition's surfaces, Folli stretched ivory canvas over wooden frames. Information about each piece on show was then printed directly onto the canvas surface. This way, the frames could support the designs they were describing and be easily rearranged as needed for different locations.

A light pink hue gives continuity to the sprawling and fragmented exhibition space

Directly speaking to the power and timelessness of Le Corbusier and Charlotte Perriand's works, La Luce was illuminated exclusively by re-editions of the original designs.

VITAMIN E eschews the digital in favour of a vibrant, three-dimensional paper theatre to promote sustainability

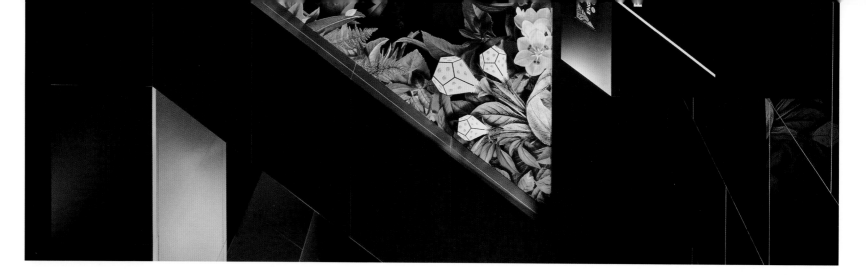

1   The base colour scheme of the stand took on a monochrome black, yet featured a striking textural contrast between the matte melamine boards of the structure and the high-gloss finish of the floors.

2   Outside the 'new sustainable world of e-mobility' the stand presented Opel's merchandise collection and the Adam.

2

PARIS — For the premier of Ampera-e, one of the world's longest-range electric cars, German automobile manufacturer Opel took a decidedly modest though no less spectacular approach to its presence at the 2016 Paris Motor Show. The future of sustainable transportation cannot be truly revolutionary without democratising its means, an ideology which studio Vitamin E made apparent in its innovative booth design.

Digital elements such as VR devices and LED screens that would ordinarily be used to signify the technological advancement of the product were eschewed in favour of one of the oldest forms of storytelling: perspective theatre. In the midst of an imposing, theatrical architecture, recesses were carved into a large, black parallelogram structure and layered with backlit graphic textiles to form vibrant dioramas. The predominant natural imagery evoked the environmentally-conscious aspect of Opel's vision of 'e-mobility' and was complemented by a tiered floor of green turf on the opposite side of the room, where visitors could socialise and view the entire three-dimensional mural.

To complete the space, a mechanical game involving racing Opel's cars from London to the Paris Motor Show was built into the structure to illustrate the 500 km range of the Ampera-e in a playful and interactive yet informative way.

156   GRAND STAND 6

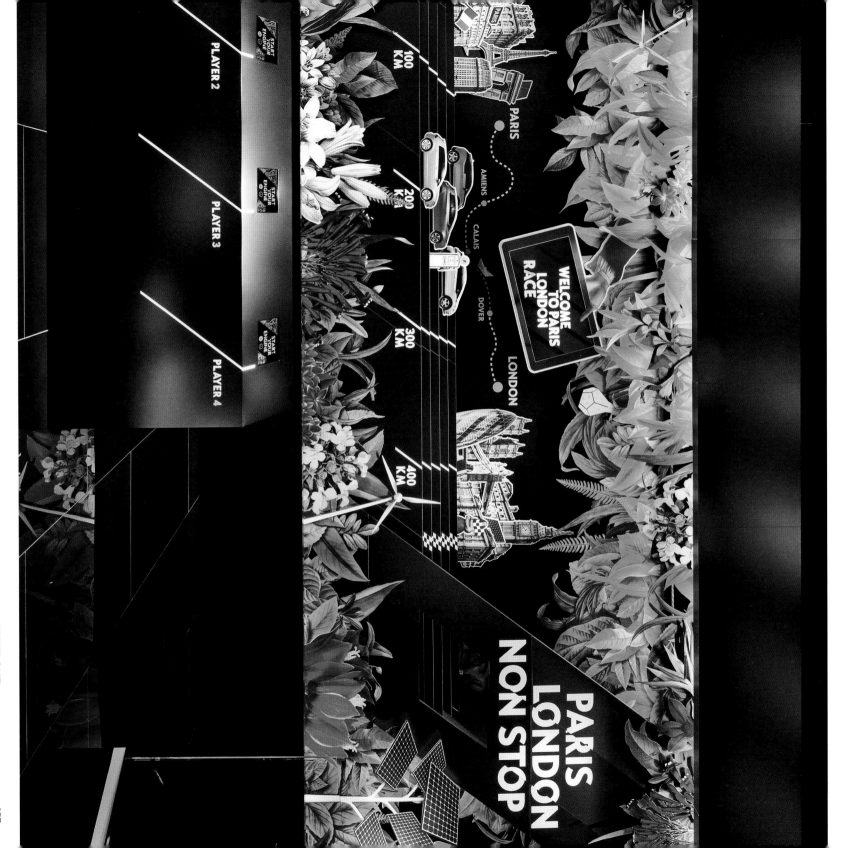

Perspective theatre, one of the oldest forms of storytelling, replaces VR devices and LED screens

Dorell.Ghotmeh.Tane

PIAGET

TSUYOSHI TANE illuminates a company's heritage of elegance and prestige

GENEVA — However simple and mundane this object might initially seem, the history of Swiss luxury watch company Piaget could not be told without the chain. Having realised this, Paris-based designer Tsuyoshi Tane explored the aesthetic potential of this component and its significance to Piaget's identity in a lavish stand at the 2016 edition of SIHH.

Alluding to the brand's tradition in watch and jewellery making, the space was surfaced in a dark blue velvety fabric, at once referencing the interior of a jewellery box and the colours used in Piaget's branding. As visitors entered the room, a night sky filled with stars materialised in the form of a dazzling array of suspended silver chains illuminated by bright downlights.

Three types of chains were used, from a thin, ball-bearing type, to a heavier, disc-filled chain. These were hung from the ceiling on both ends, forming a parabola. Their rhythmic alternation in length from just under one meter to just under three, culminated in a central, chandelier-like projection downward that partly occupied the visitors' space, thus blurring the boundary between earthly and celestial.

On the floor, marking the centre of the room, a circular, black, high-gloss panel reflected the sky of silver chains, resulting in a surreal, elegant effect that further contributed to the jewellery box imagery.

Around 14,000 metal chains, totalling a length of more than 60 km, made up the stand's starry night sky.

SIMONSWERK

GAMBIT draws on expressions of movement for reflection on innovation and tradition in door fitting products

MUNICH – The extensive collaboration between marketing and communication studio Gambit and Simonswerk included the development of a new slogan for the German door fittings brand: 'hinge systems in motion'. The opening and closing of doors are not the only movements that hinges enable. They also catalyse transition, as both a spatial and psychological phenomenon. A stand design for Simonswerk at BAU 2017 explored different expressions of movement in the context of the company's history, spanning more than 125 years, and its diverse product line.

Two large portals rose laterally from the 140 m² floor plan with contrasting exterior and interior surfaces in black and natural wood tones. The structures created the enclosing effect of a wall and ceiling while permitting circulation around the exhibition area and transparency to the exhibition hall. Beneath each archway, perpendicularly arranged tables for meetings mimicked the shape of the portals.

Taking centre stage between the two portals was a 7.5 × 1.5 m workbench like those still used in Simonswerk's production, conveying the company's ongoing commitment to craftsmanship in addition to its visionary ideas. The bench served as a spacious and comprehensive platform for the brand's sub-labels, where visitors could engage in a direct, hands-on experience of the products.

SIMONSWERK
BANDTECHNIK

Bandsysteme von SIMONSWERK für
Objekt-, Wohnraum- und Haustüren
Hinge systems from SIMONSWERK for
heavy-duty, residential and entrance doors

Unsere Marken
Bandsysteme · Made in Germany

Our Brands
Hinge Systems · Made in Germany

TECTUS®
VARIANT®
BAKA®
SIKU®
ALPRO®

Andreas Keller

SMART

BRAUNWAGNER
updates an automotive brand's stand for a new era with a digital identity

Longitudinal strips of black, tarmac-like paving contrasted with the surrounding sheen. Their staggered markings dramatically conveyed the blur of speeding down a motorway, which was complemented above by the motion of an S-shaped deck.

GENEVA — In its decade-long collaboration with smart, Braunwagner has helped the automobile company cultivate a distinctive brand presence. At the 2017 Geneva International Motor Show, the designers created a stand that reflected the company's new digital orientation and gave special emphasis to its electric drive model range.

The designers' long-lasting relationship with the brand allowed them to come to a straightforward solution that reflected smart's effort to 'go digital': they gave the distinctive booth a technological update. According to Brauwagner, 'many architectural key features of past stands were transformed into digital and media communication.'

A full-height LED screen backdrop overlaid with an illuminated matrix of dots created a complex interplay between light and media. In the foreground, dichromatic foil was applied to the front of the two information desks, in combination with graphic elements like buildings, windows and lanes. These features come to life by reflecting the LED screens dynamic output, as did the polished surfaces of the cars themselves. The digital aspect of the exhibit hence effectively unified its elements into a cohesive spectacle.

SPOTIFY

BENZ & ZIEGLER transposes
graphic design elements into a
three-dimensional stand architecture

COLOGNE – Spotify's presence at the 2015 edition of DMEXCO reflected a simple but radical rebranding strategy for its services in the digital marketing sector. Conceived by Benz & Ziegler, the Spotify for Brands booth incorporated the company's graphic design elements of bursting shapes into its architecture, using them to separate the functions of the space.

The design juxtaposed bold, geometric forms with a restrained colour palette to form a dynamic yet calming environment. The surfaces of the booth were partitioned diagonally into clean, discrete regions of green, black and white, and counterbalanced by rectangular furnishings. Grey triangles were set against each other and projected at alternating angles from the background and the ceiling, creating a striking three-dimensional effect and conveying motion and emergence.

Standing in contrast to the stand's geometric backdrop, tables and seating featured untreated wood surfaces interspersed with greenery. The soft, organic quality of these elements in the midst of the futuristic setting reminded visitors of the ubiquity of Spotify, a service that can be used in the most remote and natural settings. Their strange harmony with the surrounding architecture signified a unity between nature and virtual space brought about by Spotify – 'there is music everywhere.'

Thomas Stefan

VAUDE

ATELIER 522
plants seeds of sustainability with a monumental tree-inspired installation

MUNICH – Dissatisfied with the lack of standardised tests for product eco-friendliness, German outdoor clothing and gear brand Vaude developed Green Shape, their own system of rigorous sustainability evaluation criteria. For their booth at the 2017 edition of sporting trade fair ISPO, Vaude commissioned atelier 522 to transform the metrics of Green Shape into a three-dimensional experience and a compelling brand message.

The centrepiece of the stand was an abstract tree installation comprised of green climbing ropes that extended up in the cylindrical form of a narrow trunk and draped out to form a canopy over the entire exhibition space. At the end of each rope, a carabiner held a single leaf that read 'Vaude Green Shape'. An assertive presence yet with a delicate composition, the tree embodied the dichotomy between the power and fragility of nature.

To complete the stand, the installation was surrounded by a bare wood frame carved out with narrow alcoves that shelter casual meeting areas. Along the frame, illuminated, rectangular display areas featured highlights from the brand's latest collection while providing insight into the recycled materials and ethical production processes in their origins.

VAUDE
GREEN SHAPE
GUARANTEED VAUDE ECO PRODUCT
VAUDE Green Shape
Schau Dir unseren Green Shape Film an!
Green Shape
For (y)our world worth living in.

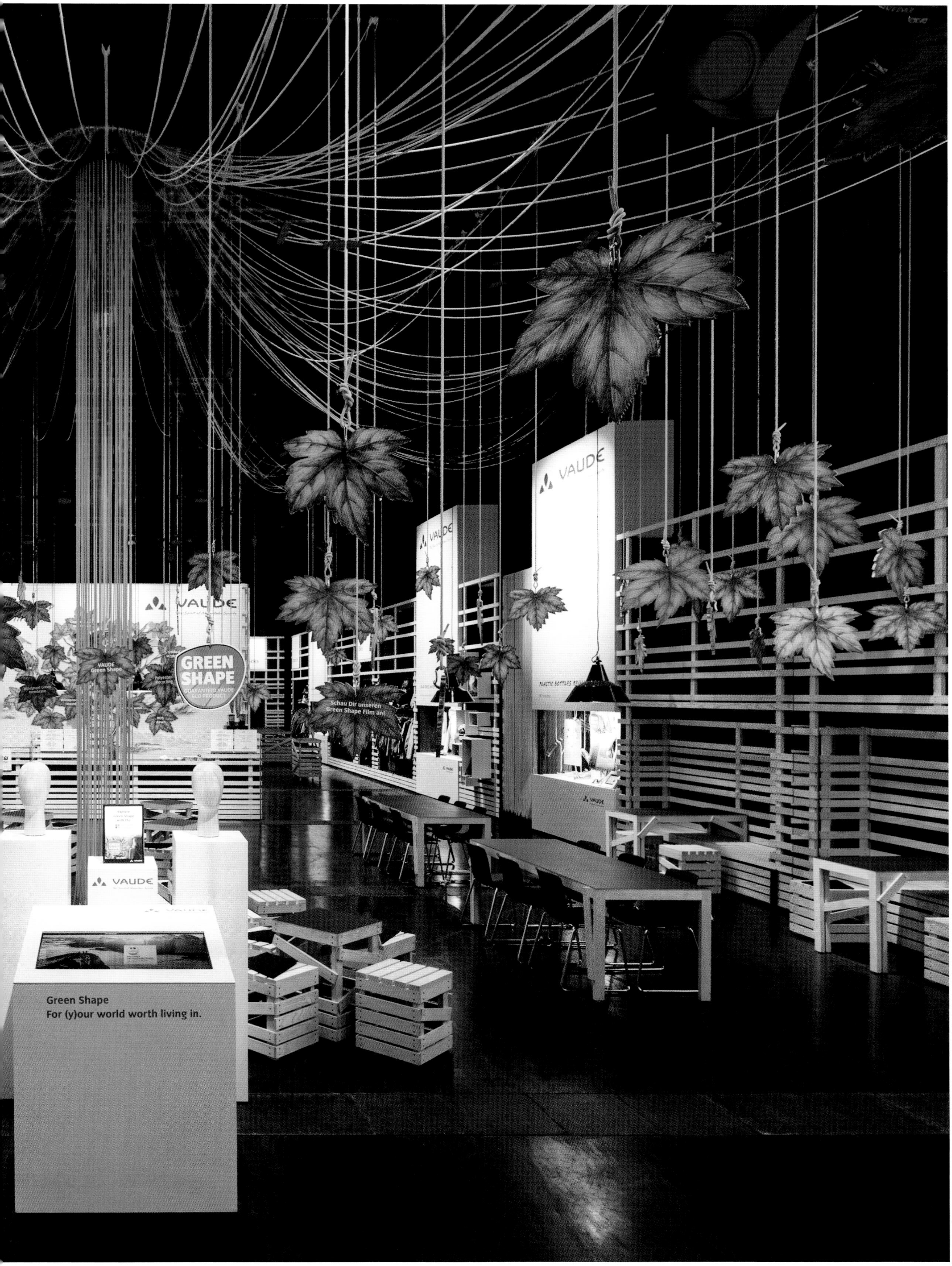

DUSSELDORF — Studio D'art Design Gruppe realised a joint appearance for the German Pulp and Paper Association and the Federal Association for Print and Media at Drupa 2016. With the objective of conveying the symbiotic relationship between the agencies' respective specialties — paper and print — Dart created an emotive, three-dimensional experience of these media and offered a vision for their future.

The 180 m² exhibition space was mostly covered in a bare, monochrome white, with sparse furnishings for lounging, conversation and reflection. Dividing the square diagonally, a 3.5-m-high sculpture comprised the words 'print' and 'paper' placed back-to-back, both cast in a

clean, simple, yet bold and modern sans-serif font. The word 'paper' was wrapped in white paper to match the surfaces of the booth, while the word 'print' showcased a vibrant collage consisting of publications representative of almost all printing techniques.

Each created a stage out of the space in front of it for their respective associations, and with both words literally embodying their antecedent and juxtaposed against the other, the visitor was compelled to consider the various interactions between print and paper. In the midst of the rapid changes occurring in these industries, the booth was well-received as a rejuvenating catalyst for speculation on their enduring possibilities.

Lukas Palik

VDP

DART
invites
reflection
on the
symbiotic
relationship
between
paper and
print

Placed in one corner of the stand, the cubic
information desk was shared between the
two protagonists.

WICONA

ATELIER SEITZ opens a window to the future of the metropolis

At a height of up to 7.5 m, red bolts ensured that the stand could not to be missed.

MUNICH – At BAU 2015, visitors had experienced the Wicona City of the present (Grand Stand 5, p.068-069). Two years later, at BAU 2017, longtime collaborator Atelier Seitz, presented the Wicona City of the future through a new stand design. The stand highlighted the company's innovative window, door and facade systems by creating a daring and futuristic spectacle of the metropolis to come.

Angled grey walls irregularly intersecting each other at once framed the booth space, and served as the display for highlight products. Oversized red bolts likened these masses to planks at a construction site, while their weightless, immaterial appearance depicted motion, resulting in an imagery of an urban landscape in the process of forming. Civic archetypes such as printed skylines, pedestrians, road markings, and birds further anchored this structure in recognisable signifiers and brought the imagined city to life.

In the middle of the 648 m² booth, an 'esplanade' featured two abstract trees comprising buoyant clusters of coloured aluminium bars, contrasting with the surrounding two-tone colour scheme. Benches and stools surrounding these trees invited visitors to pause and contemplate. An adjacent exhibition space contained a three-dimensional model of a fictitious city, which aggregated notable international buildings that feature Wicona products. With the aid of tablet devices, visitors could take a virtual tour of this model town.

A daring and
futuristic spectacle
of the metropolis
to come

GEMEINSAM die Stadt
der Zukunft GESTALTEN

HELLER DESIGNSTUDIO's booth for Mercedes-Benz Energy invites visitors to experience the future of sustainable power

MUNICH — A new sub-brand of the iconic Swabian car maker, Mercedes-Benz Energy demanded a monumental debut at the 2016 Intersolar energy technology fair. Stuttgart-based Heller Designstudio responded with a bold, architectonic structure that showcased the sustainable future Mercedes' subsidiary could make possible with its wide range of products.

The cubic, two-story booth consisted of a closed black volume hovering over a permeable, ground-floor exhibition area. Floors and ceilings with reflective foil surfaces were broken into a grid by pulsating LED lines, which symbolised the flow of energy. A sci-fi ambience which recalled the digital landscape in Tron was counterbalanced by organic materials that asserted renewability and environmental awareness.

Setting the scene for the energy storage product, climbing plants filled the space of the ground floor to create a jungle-like environment. Suspended from light boxes, the greenery partially hedged off the exhibition within, inciting the onlooker's curiosity to discover what was inside. Ascending into the enigmatic volume above, visitors encountered a dark, secluded room with private meeting areas and additional displays, for which a screen projecting animations formed a dynamic backdrop.

Furniture icons by Danish design company Fritz Hansen invoked the classic elegance of the Mercedes-Benz brand identity.

SPACON & X designs a raw mood board to highlight the prolific portfolio of a fashion brand

COPENHAGEN – Wood Wood's subcultural roots have flourished in the arenas of streetwear and sportswear just as much as high fashion. The young Danish label's presence at Copenhagen Fashion Week 2017, realised by Spacon & X, sought to broaden the brand identity in order to reflect its diverse and prolific portfolio.

Danish studio Spacon & X chose to strip back Wood Wood's presentation to a 'work-in-progress' state, inviting visitors to step into the macrocosm of a mood board. Untreated MDF, concrete, stretch metal, pinewood poles and brick assembled in bare, haphazard configurations formed a simple material vocabulary. MDF boards and concrete created a flexible, modular

rack system for the clothing, adjustable for different pieces and adaptable to subsequent venues.

A colour palette of pastel blues and reds softened the rawness of these elements, culminating in the vibrant flecks of the Everroll rubber floor. Mirrored steel surfaces, sheets of glass and hand-painted rocks added a refined contrast to the setting, representing creativity in its later stages of development. By using a representation of the creative process as the backdrop for the end result, the designers created an unusual yet compelling synergy that communicated to visitors coherently the wild and dexterous complexity of Wood Wood's line.

1 Raw elements such as bricks were juxtaposed against artificial renderings of themselves as a representation of the booth's dialogue between art and reality.

2 The mirrored steel surfaces of certain fixtures created playful distortions of space that elevated the realism of the exhibit.

GRAND STAND 6

Spacon & X invites visitors to step into the macrocosm of a mood board

ZANAT

NORMAL ARHITEKTURA
weaves a company's history into a resplendent ceiling sculpture

COLOGNE — Commissioned to develop a stand for a century-old company with a 2-years-old brand, Sarajevo-based studio normal arhitektura felt compelled to delve into the history of Zanat, a UNESCO nominee for intangible cultural heritage. The brief called for an outstanding, inexpensive design and that's exactly what the studio delivered at IMM Cologne 2016, bringing to the spotlight the longstanding traditions of, until then, a little known brand.

The design began with a traditional Bosnian rug, the Kilim, with which one of Zanat's antique chairs was upholstered. Using a sample from its pattern, the designers created a pixelated flying carpet over the exhibition space. Made up of 3025 wooden cubes extending from the ceiling in an undulating pattern, the result is a mesmerizing sculpture into which the heritage of the company was weaved and presented as a relevant and enticing experience to contemporary audiences.

Built and assembled by Zanat carpenters, the 'carpet' also functions as an example of the company's capabilities as well as the myriad possibilities of its raw material: wood. Beneath this majestic spectacle, Zanat's products were displayed on a platform of plain, white surfaces or, as the designers put it, 'a simple white box, and that was enough.'

SHAPE

UP

Highlighting products
through architecture

FABIO CALVI and PAOLO BRAMBILLA, Co-founders of Calvi Brambilla, go straight to the point on the challenges and particularities of an architectural approach to stand design.

Helenio Barbetta

'The design should guide visitors to focus on the products, not the stand'

What do you think is the biggest challenge in stand design? For us, it is to respond to many different needs and to respect a lot of constraints. One of the prevailing constraints is time. All the choices must be made quickly, we must respect fair regulations and meet the client's needs while managing all costs within a strict budget. Moreover, the biggest goal is trying to push forward the barriers of the contemporary taste.

A good exhibition designer is an architect, a scenographer and a graphic designer with extensive hands-on experience of marketing and communication tools, but also a producer and a good manager. In fact, creativity, though essential, is a small part of the design process, the rest is finding solutions by managing the project at all stages.

How do you approach this type of projects? First we talk with our client to focus on the brand values, the new products, the target, the budget and every information that can help us. Once we have all these elements, we try to define a concept that is consistent with the brief but unexpected at the same time.

In the first *Grand Stand* the question is put forward of 'whether it is the stand that makes the running, or the contents.' How do you find the right balance between a beautiful, eye-catching stand, and one that doesn't overshadow the products on display? The design of a stand must always be perfectly consistent with what it contains, or with the brand it represents, even though fair booths have to be eye-catching to be noticed among many others. We don't like projects where the author's personal touch prevails. Especially when you're inside, the design should guide you to focus on the products, not on the stand.

How can architectural structures contribute to the products on display? They can help when you need to isolate the set from the visual pollution of a fair. Only this way you can control the quality of space and light and recreate exactly the intended atmosphere.

What are the merits of this approach to stand design? An architectural approach works only if the product scale is well managed compared to the available space.

In the case of the Flos stand, we had to show a collection of exceptionally large, iconic, monumental lighting fixtures, so we decided to design the stand as a contemporary building, the Flos building. Open spaces are somehow precarious, they soon reveal their identity instead of creating a mystery feeling and don't convey the authoritativeness of the company. Having a closed space, a layout that often the client prefers, allows to create a pavilion with its own strength and autonomy.

What are the biggest challenges when it comes to creating a rather ambitious structure like the Flos stand on what is often a restrictive budget? Any good designer is able to manage the budget assigned to a project, you don't necessarily need a lot of money to achieve a great result. At the 2017 Salone del Mobile we designed seven booths, each one with a different mood, and for each one we were able to meet the budget. We keep in mind the money we can spend from the beginning of the design process, and work with the contractors to find the less expensive solutions.

How can space and exhibition-focused stands compete with user experience-driven designs? We personally don't believe that interactivity can support the strength of a booth, especially it enhances a problem of slow flow of people. In addition, according to our experience, the request of interactive solutions such as touch screens has greatly decreased in the last few years, focusing instead on a strong concept idea. On the other hand, the need to create a content that communicates with the social networks has become fundamental. For example, in Pedrali's booth at Orgatec 2016, the concept provided isolated spaces as three-dimensional paintings on two big side walls, highly appreciated by editors and journalists because they could easily be photographed and shared on the most famous social media platforms like Instagram. Interactive solutions and technologies can in any case coexist with the architectural design approach.

Do you think trade fairs will become obsolete in the digital era? Today people can get a lot of information simply sitting on the sofa, so why should they travel the world and visit a fair? Our belief is that there is a strong demand for physical experiences even if we are now in the digital communication era, or maybe because of that. People want to know how it's like to be in a special place, with their own body, surrounded by other people experiencing the same space at the same time.

A dazzling, reflective grid by TISCH 13 showcases the technological developments of an automotive brand

LAS VEGAS — Since 2011, Audi's presence at the Consumer Electronics Show has been managed by Munich-based studio Tisch 13. Filling up to 500 m² of a grand hall, each incarnation has explored the architectural possibilities of the box. For the 2016 edition, the automotive brand wanted to showcase its increased emphasis on digital connectivity and smart technology.

Headlined by the communication banner 'Audi Intelligence', Tisch 13's dazzling response was a massive, rectilinear grid formed from over 4 km of mirrored aluminium beams joined by nodes in a dynamic configuration. The highly-polished, silver surfaces of the three-dimensional grid reflected everything in sight, with animated spotlights in and above the installation adding to the play of light, and the glossy white industrial flooring doubling the spectacle below.

Although seemingly disorienting and chaotic from afar, visitors entered the space through one of the three openings to discover a cohesive and complex structure comprising a network of interconnected layers. Described by Tisch 13 as 'reactive architecture', the stand was an immersive space in which the Audi brand came to life and the visitor became an active component of the network embodied by the display. Within the sculptural structure, exhibition spaces highlighted Audi's latest models and technological developments.

The stand's reactive architecture brings the brand to life and makes visitors one of its active components

A video screen at one end of the stand displayed a media show whose effects added to the play of light and reflections, as well as to the theme of digital technology.

Piet Albert Goethals

OFFICE deconstructs the typologies of interior, installation and furnishings with a full-scale reproduction of a villa

2

1   For his designs, muller van severen used wire mesh and volumetric objects inspired by the house's curvature and ambiguous sense of enclosure.

2   Challenging the boundaries of contemporary furniture, Richard Venlet retrofitted found stools as mobile lamps that reconfigure the lighting dynamic of the villa.

KORTRIJK — At the 2016 Biennale Interieur, a series of six installations housed in tall, perforated industrial steel plates formed miniature worlds that were part of the fair's Silver Lining: Interiors curatorial programme. One of these spaces, designed by the curators of the fair themselves, transported visitors to the sublime forests of southwest Catalonia. Nearly 1500 km away from its original setting, Brussels design studio OFFICE Kersten Geers David Van Severen created a partial 1:1 reconstruction of its Solo House in Matarranya.

The original structure, isolated on a remote plateau and cut off from all utilities, is intended to be at once invisible in relation to its surroundings, and an experiment in architecture defined only by devices. A simple circular roof defines the perimeter of the house, with four straight rows of supporting columns cutting chords into the radial floor plan. Photovoltaic panels and buffer tanks collecting and storing energy, as well as a water purifier, are arranged on the roof as abstract objects.

An arc segment of the structure was reproduced in the Kortrijk showroom, yet took on a different meaning through various artistic interventions. Artist Pieter Vermeersch, for instance, reimagined the utilities devices of the house as contemporary sculptures with subtle transformations to their colour and texture. Designers such as Richard Venlet and muller van severen crafted new furniture for the decor. This way, architecture, installation and furnishings were deliberately aggregated into one ambiguous whole, establishing a site for new spatial and functional typologies.

Architecture, installation and furnishings are deliberately aggregated into one ambiguous whole

GRAND STAND 6

JANGLED NERVES and ATELIER MARKGRAPH
deliver a holistic brand image through a spatial choreography

FRANKFURT — Mercedes-Benz once again took over the century-old Frankfurt Festival Hall for the city's 2015 International Motor Show. Beneath the hall's majestic dome, over 9000 m² of display area covering three levels showcased the diversity of the car maker's latest offerings and incorporated a new, yet familiar and highly-lauded spatial brand concept, developed by Jangled Nerves (architecture) and Atelier Markgraph (communication).

Several exhibition areas each with a distinct style that mirrored its theme wrapped around the two upper galleries of the arena, which overlooked a broad main stage. Visitors began the expedition through the world of Mercedes-Benz by ascending a grand escalator to the top floor and worked their way down, guided by the brand's signature Silver Flow. This sculptural,

all-encompassing spatial element comprised 400 strips of reflective aluminium, each with a custom position, tilt and rotation. Together, the strips formed a dynamic, three-dimensional stream that was brought to life by animated, coloured lighting, and cast different moods and atmosphere throughout the entire space.

The serpentine path of the Silver Flow descended from the ceiling and seamlessly ran into the LED screen behind the stage. The screen itself was made of individual strips that, like blinds, rotated to reveal a colossal, three-storey shelving unit, which displayed vehicles from the new collections. Shows on the stage coordinated the display elements with performers, car tests and live video sequences, creating a sensory choreography of the brand image.

A sculptural, three-dimensional stream is brought to life by animated, coloured lighting

Weltpremiere

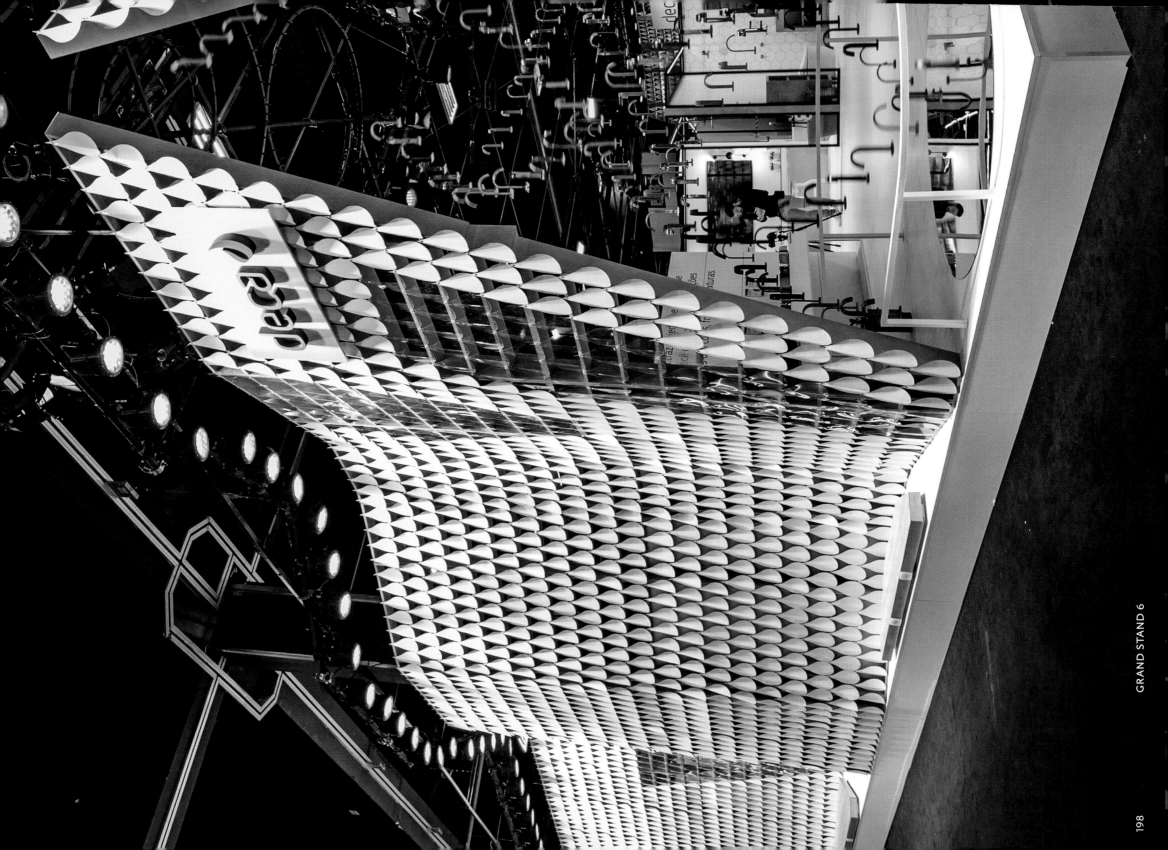

DECA AND HYDRA

An elaborate, shimmering facade by GTM **CENOGRAFIA** envelops two brands in a cohesive presentation

Nearly 10,000 paper and crystal acrylic drop-shaped elements make up the facade

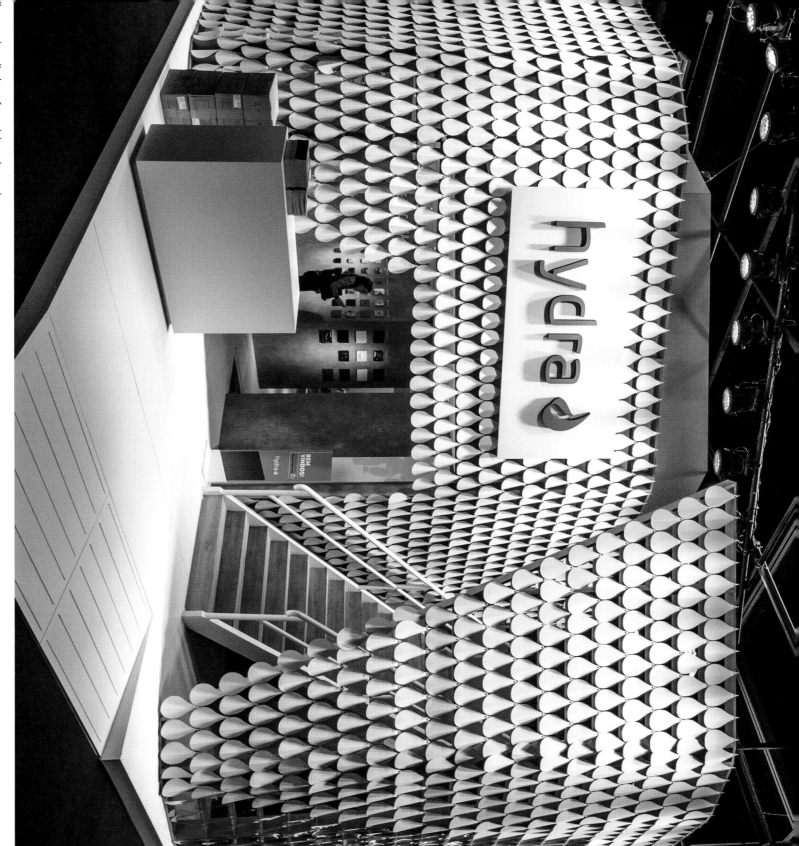

The crystal acrylic drops formed dynamic, angular
punctures in the facade.

SÃO PAULO – For the third consecutive year,
local scenic designer and constructor GTM
Cenografia was commissioned to construct a
stand for affiliated brands Deca and Hydra at the
2017 Expo Revestir. As with previous designs, the
companies' sanitary wares demanded a lasting
and grandiose impact that would showcase their
latest improvements and capabilities.

The concept began with a feature common
to all of Deca's and Hydra's products – a drop
of water. A modular facade consisted of nearly
10,000 paper and crystal acrylic drop-shaped
elements. The folded paper drops produced
shimmer and movement across the surface, while
the transparent acrylic material and the natural

voids created between the units allowed for light,
ventilation and transparency. The floor plan,
though divided into two blocks for each brand,
was visually unified by the facade's continuous
texture.

At the heart of the booth, four bathroom
environments were arranged on a swivel floor
that allowed each display to be viewed from
any point in the interior. Similarly, a rotating
sculpture of faucets showcased the variety
of available colours and finishes. An open
mezzanine area with a bar, lounge and meeting
rooms afforded visitors a view over the entire
exhibition space.

DESIGNPLUS and **SPACE ENCOUNTERS**
build an architectural carousel to convey
a multifaceted identity

1

Peter Tijhuis

DUSSELDORF — Stuttgart-based studio Designplus presented itself at EuroShop 2017 with a booth conceived in partnership with Dutch architects Space Encounters. Through a daring and playful installation, the design team conveyed the manifold character and portfolio of the atelier while reaffirming its primary fascination with space in the creation of a brand experience.

The display comprised a circular sculpture on a raised platform partitioned into six sections. Made entirely of chipboard and cast in a muted sage, its simplified chromatic and material palette shifted the visitors' attention onto the conceptual aspects of the experience. Each of the six zones embodied an archetypal space — portal, temple,

conference, factory, store and capsule — that represented some aspect of the company's culture and philosophy.

A prominent phrase found on the exterior, 'Join the ride!', hinted at the unusual mechanism within the stand. Once inside, visitors discovered that the centre rotated to form new spatial configurations. When this happened, the textual elements on the walls were rearranged to generate new phrases. The aggregate effect was a bold statement of flexibility and the desire to form new architectural typologies through brand narrative. At the same time, a disco ball at the carousel's core added a touch of humour and whim to the studio's image.

Rotating rooms form new spatial and textual configurations, conveying flexibility

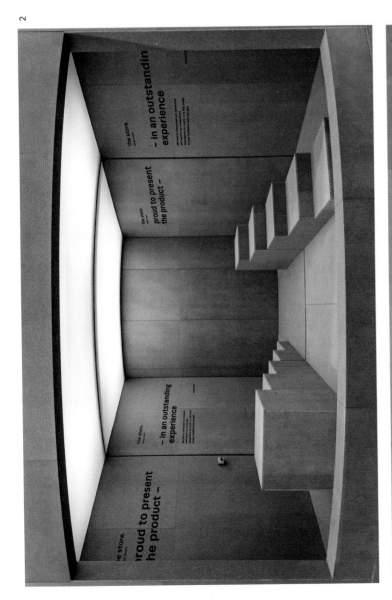

1 A separate rectangular mass portraying a ticket booth to the carousel served as a satellite stand for the launch of the first edition of Designplus Collaboration Journal.

2 The stand's rotating mechanism allowed for 36 different spatial combinations, each with its unique message.

IPPOLITO FLEITZ GROUP reveals the stylistic potential of flooring by turning a display inside out

nueller

MUNICH — DLW Flooring considers BAU its most important channel for communicating with consumers and has consequently built a tradition of creating an exceptional and memorable presence at the fair. The company's 2017 exhibition was no exception: a dynamic, open and engaging spatial concept by Ippolito Fleitz Group.

The challenge with promoting flooring solutions is always asserting its potential as a stylistic instrument rather than simply an architectural necessity. Under the theme 'Inside Out', Ippolito Fleitz Group's design achieved just that by enveloping the stand in a shell that dissolved or receded to reveal the variety of colour and texture in DLW's products. These plain, white partitions formed a bare sketch of the exterior, with large voids carved out to create a light and porous interior. The atmosphere suggested the transparency of the company's values, committed not only to high aesthetic standards but also minimising its environmental footprint.

The circular and semi-circular segments cut out from the walls were covered in vibrant collages of DLW flooring products and set back into the walls at an angle, or as rotating disks. This way, the design offered a haptic experience of the products to visitors, whose interaction with the stand resulted in continually changing perspectives. The energetic play of form and colour culminated in the vibrant back walls, where the flooring products formed large, geometric compositions that created a 'permanent stage set for this dance of forms and colours,' the architects say.

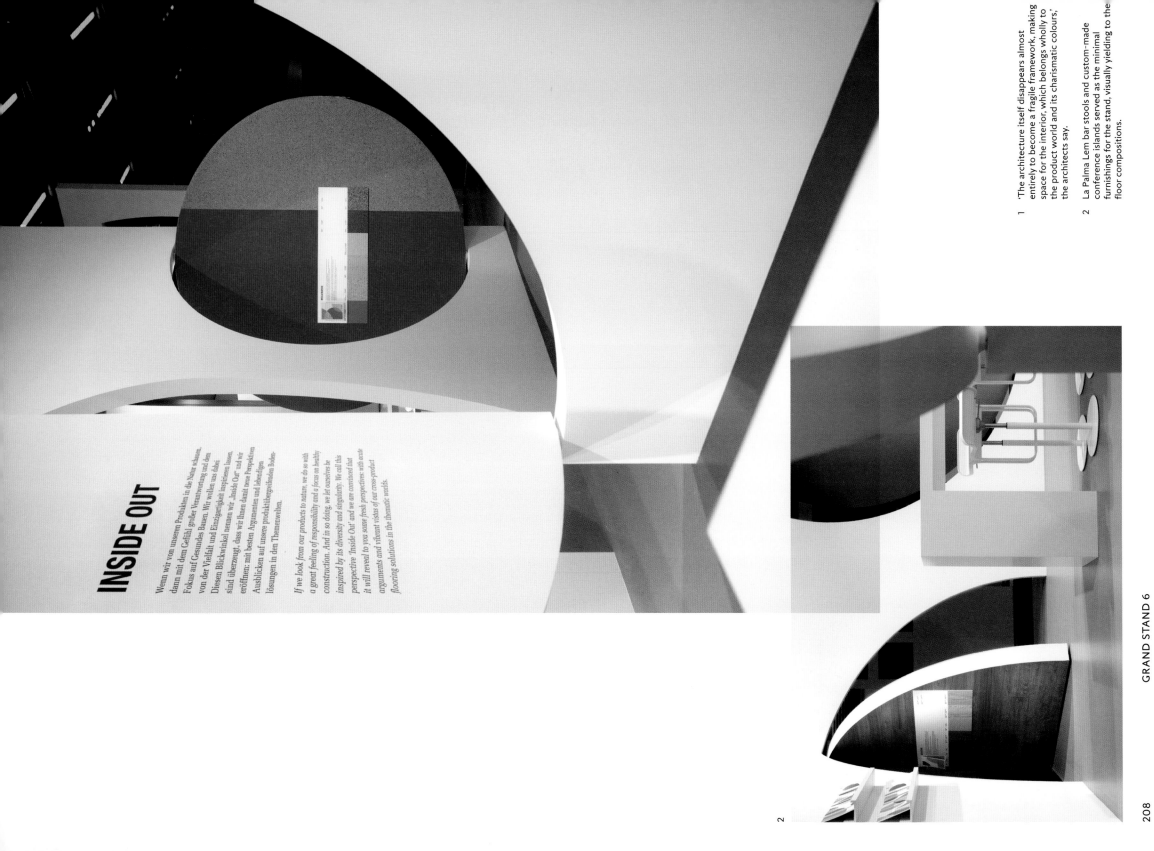

INSIDE OUT

Wenn wir von unseren Produkten in die Natur schauen, dann mit dem Gefühl großer Verantwortung und dem Fokus auf Gesundes Bauen. Wir wollen uns dabei von der Vielfalt und Einzigartigkeit inspirieren lassen. Diesen Blickwinkel nennen wir ,Inside Out' und wir eröffnen: mit besten Argumenten und lebendigen Ausblicken auf unsere produktübergreifenden Bodenlösungen in den Themenwelten.

If we look from our products to nature, we do so with a great feeling of responsibility and a focus on healthy construction. And in so doing, we let ourselves be inspired by its diversity and singularity. We call this perspective 'Inside Out' and we are convinced that it will reveal to you some fresh perspectives with acute arguments and vibrant vistas of our cross-product flooring solutions in the thematic worlds.

1   'The architecture itself disappears almost entirely to become a fragile framework, making space for the interior, which belongs wholly to the product world and its charismatic colours,' the architects say.

2   La Palma Lem bar stools and custom-made conference islands served as the minimal furnishings for the stand, visually yielding to the floor compositions.

Large, geometric compositions create a permanent stage set for a dance of forms and colours

ATELIER MARKO BRAJOVIC
unfolds the ozone trioxide molecule into a dome-shaped booth

SÃO PAULO - Visitors to the 2017 edition of Expo Revestir may not have imagined they were entering the realm of the microscopic when they stumbled upon the otherworldly booth for Brazilian faucet company Docol. To promote DocolVitalis, a new tap system that emits activated oxygen water, São Paulo-based firm Atelier Marko Brajovic took inspiration from the ozone trioxide molecule, the key feature of this technology.

Three contiguous geodesic domes represented the three oxygen atoms of the molecule's chemical composition. Their metal structures were patterned after a Voronoi diagram (a naturally-occurring geometric modulation that is found in water bubbles) and

their translucent voids distorted the outside light to provide a surreal, immersive experience.

Each of the domes provided a different multi-sensory experience that contextualised the visitor into a specific aspect of the technology. A laboratory featuring the faucets themselves explained the science behind the mechanism; a central dome with fog and sound-responsive lights emulated the system's cleansing process; and a futuristic greenhouse represented the greener world which the technology could help create. Collectively, they formed a coherent and powerful spatial narrative. As an experimental architecture and possible future habitat, Atelier Marko Brajovic's design effectively became part of Docol's vision for the future.

2

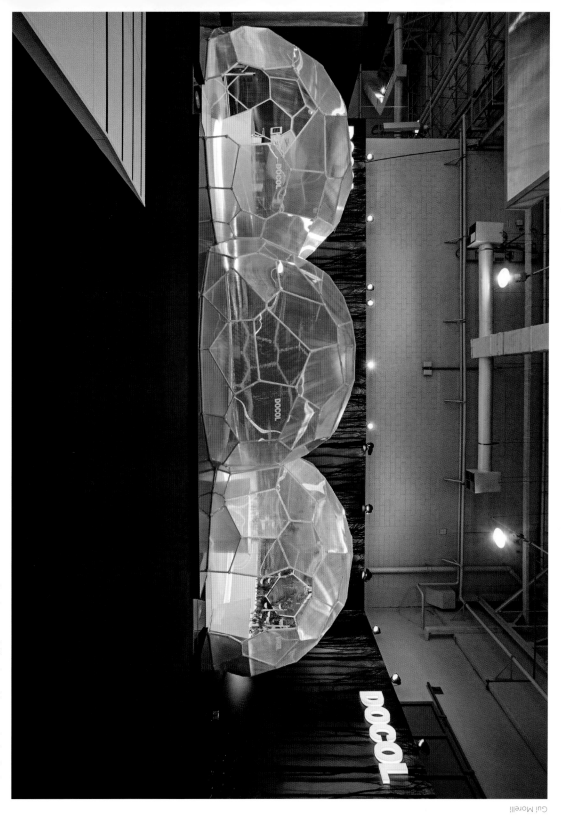

1 A recessed, illuminated base made the display appear to hover, contributing to the booth's futuristic aesthetic.

2 Plants in the greenhouse were suspended in test tubes and flasks, a solution that helped to visually and conceptually connect this section with the laboratory dome.

Gui Morelli

DONGPENG

A stand design by VXLAB brings together a company's timeless elegance and technological innovation

BOLOGNA — As the largest and best-selling ceramics manufacturer in China, Dongpeng sought to expand its reputation on an international level. For its presentation at Cersaie 2016, the company commissioned Spanish studio VXLab to create an image accessible to Western audiences and translate its vision for the future while preserving its 45-year heritage.

VXLab took the nature of light as inspiration for its design, constructing an enigmatic booth that appeared as if a secret waiting for visitors to unveil. A cubic shell featured a backlit facade that emanated an inviting and striking glow in the midst of the showroom. The company's logo stood out in a reflective silver against this radiant backdrop.

The design's exploration of the nature of light continued inside with prominent use of pendant lighting. Entering through a singular geometric void, one encountered an ethereal white room with floors and walls paved in Dongpeng's marble-effect tiles. The hexagonal mosaic on the floor broke up the space's rectilinear shape and gracefully interacted with the ceramic slabs on the walls and display boxes, conveying the timeless elegance of the brand.

A backlit facade emanates an inviting and striking glow in the midst of the showroom

1   Individual hexagon tiles were raised from the floor at varying heights to produce a three dimensional effect.

2   Stylised copy such as 'The future is inspiring' and 'Where technology meets art' connected Dongpeng's products with an identity of progressive innovation.

WHERE TECHNOLOGY
MEETS ART

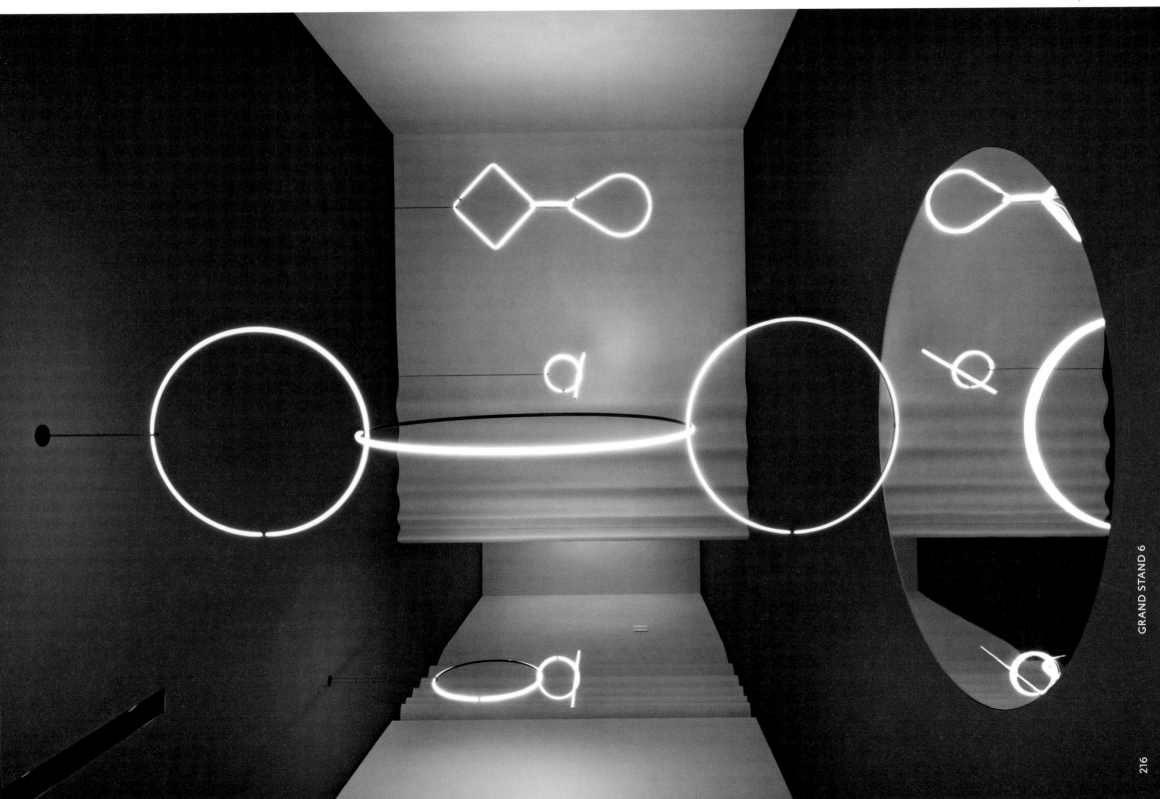

Within a stern and imposing monolith by CALVI BRAMBILLA lies a world of light

MILAN – Calvi Brambilla collaborated once again with Flos on a stand for the 2017 edition of Salone del Mobile's Euroluce exposition. The Italian lighting company required a large-scale and emotional debut for a variety of new products and systems within its home, architectural and outdoor collections. In a space covering over 1000 m², the studio articulated a minimalist yet dynamic series of scenes in which the luminaires became the leading actors.

A double-height rectangular volume cast in a monochrome grey created a colossal and monolithic spectacle in the exhibition hall. Bringing the mass to life, walls on both the exterior and interior rarefied seamlessly into accordion-like curtains. Inside, ascetic staging and reflective surfaces gave the products an active and mystical presence within the display.

The studio's last concept for Flos in 2011 had used vibrant shades of orange and exposed building materials to suggest that it was still 'under construction'. Though the quiet minimalism of the 2017 stand may have seemed completely divergent, it was actually an extension of this theme. Rather than serving as a static container for the exhibition, the structure created a happening around the Flos brand, in which the company's lighting actively constructed spatial perception.

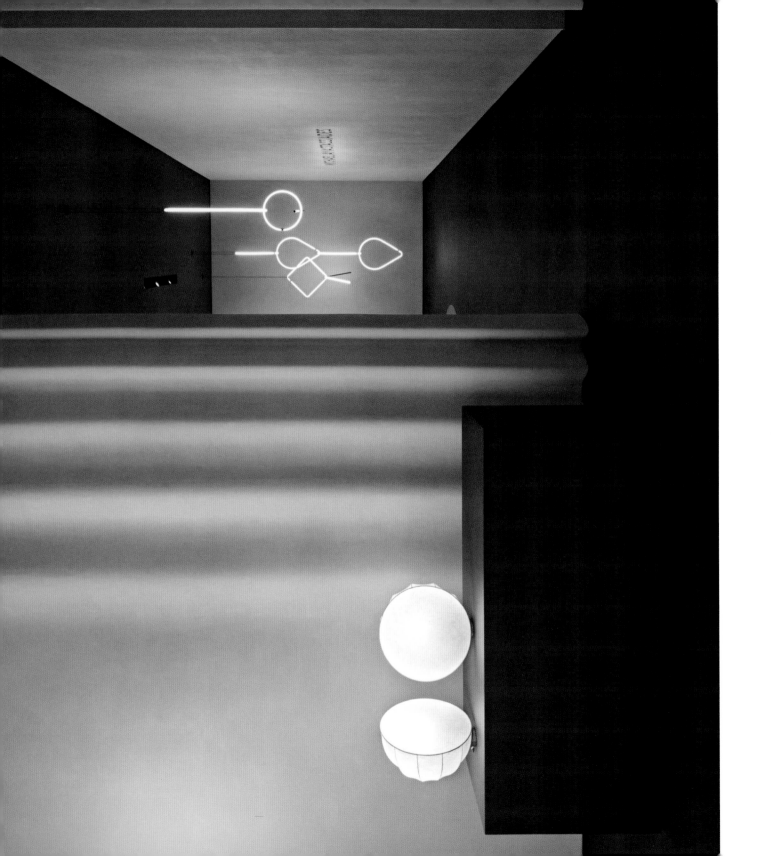

Ascetic staging and reflective surfaces give the products an active and mystical presence within the display

The stand interior was interspersed with greenery that flowed between passages, blurring the distinction between inside and outside.

Mirrors placed at different orientations distorted the perception of space in the otherwise stark interiors.

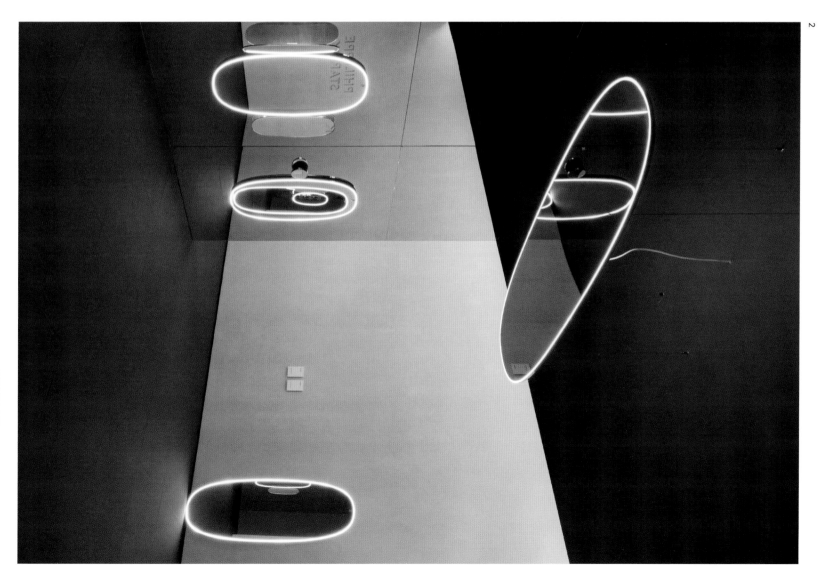

2

GENESIS MANNEQUINS

BLOCHER PARTNERS illustrates the potential of mannequins in an origami-inspired exhibition space

Four mirror elements multiply a tree's delicate branches and immerse the visitor in a surreal forest

The 700 m² space logged more than 10,000 registered visitors and was nominated for the AMAB award.

DUSSELDORF – Mannequins are perhaps more likely to be perceived as an installation art cliché than a fixture of the retail experience in an era dominated by e-commerce. Genesis Mannequins, a major international player in the industry, sought to cast a light of creative and technological potential in the midst of physical retail's decline, with a booth at EuroShop 2017 that ultimately proved to be one of the fair's most popular for that year.

Realised by Stuttgart-based design team Blocher Partners, the angular, monochrome white exhibition space appeared like a giant mass of folded paper. The company's graceful figures lined the inner walls of this origami world, representing the diversity of twelve product lines: classic and futuristic, stationary and moveable, otherworldly and lifelike. Defining the centre of the space, an abstract tree extended its geometric branches in every direction. The sculpture evoked the environmental awareness of the brand's products, all manufactured from a sustainably-generated bio resin. Four mirror elements were placed at cardinal positions around the tree, multiplying the delicate branches and immersing the visitor in a surreal forest. Drawing further into the Genesis world, VR glasses demonstrated new technologies implemented by the company in production, including virtual sculpting and 3D printing.

223

FÖRSTBERG LING reveals the layers of an office furniture brand through a sequence of translucent screens

STOCKHOLM – Presented with the Editor's Choice award at the 2017 Stockholm Furniture Fair, Kinnarps's booth resulted from a close collaboration between the Swedish company's creative director Johan Ronnestam and Malmö-based studio Förstberg Ling. To implement a new brand platform, Kinnarps requested a display that would create a closed environment while still allowing outsiders a glimpse of the activity within.

'The Silhouettes of Kinnarps' was Förstberg Ling's answer. Translucent partitions made of glulam columns and voile fabric formed the walls of the stand, revealing only the outlines of the furniture displays behind them. A route led visitors

through distinct exhibition areas, each separated by a layer of transparency. Located on either end of the stand, at the entrances, the monochromatic displays evoked enticing colour schemes and stood out boldly against the structure's uniform cerulean.

At the centre, a two-story volume housed meeting areas and additional exhibition space on the ground floor and a bar on the first floor. From this more secluded and contemplative space, one could visualise the entire booth, giving visitors a holistic outlook which unified the tenets of the brand message. The centremost tower, an open, vertical space, was dedicated to Kinnarps' 75th anniversary, hosting a presentation that chronicled the brand's history and promoted its future.

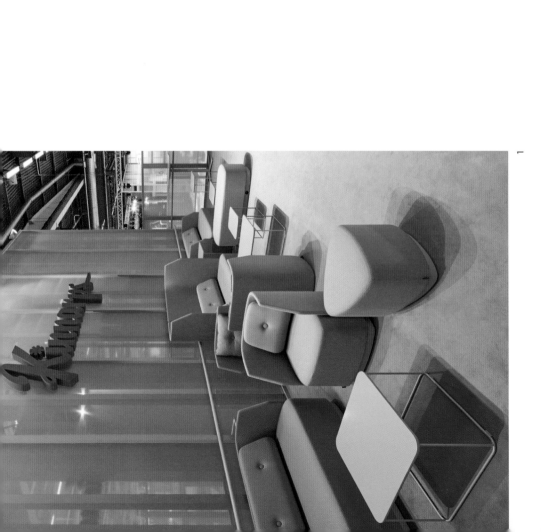

Translucent partitions reveal the silhouettes of the furniture displays behind them

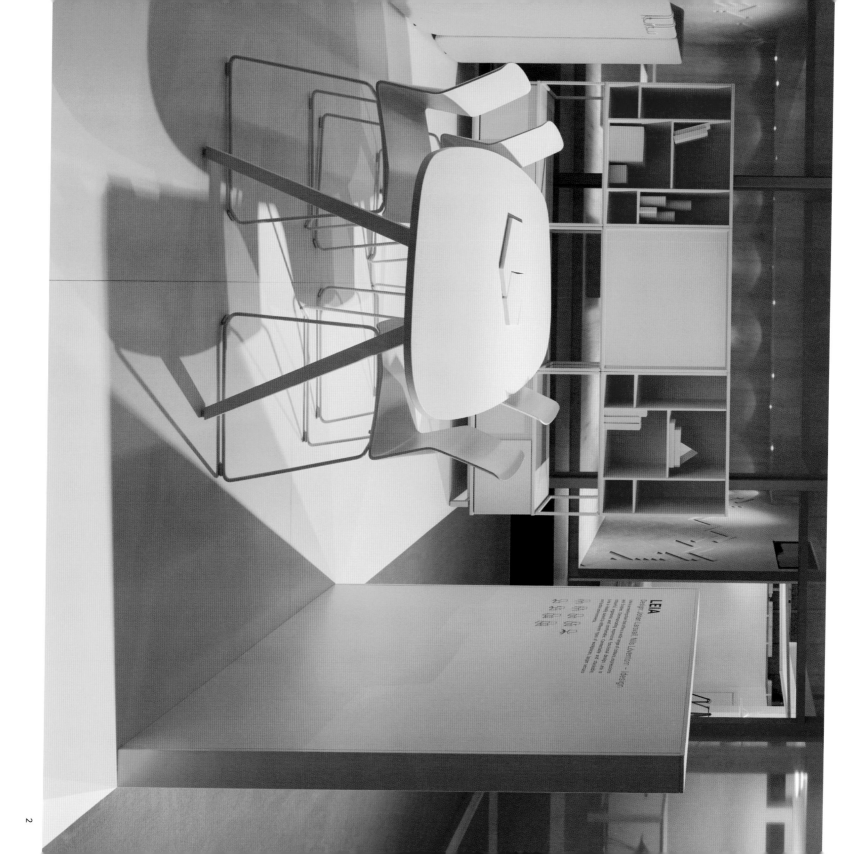

Furniture on the first floor bar took on the structure's blue tone, allowing visitors to experience the surreal atmosphere of the displays below.

The rectilinear construction of the stand created a sleek, simple and streamlined canvas for emphasis on colour and transparency.

LEIA
Design: Jonas Lindvall, Nola Lidström – design

2

KREON

KRISTOF PYCKE uses spatial design to reveal the functionality of lighting products

FRANKFURT – Belgian lighting company Kreon sought to showcase the natural functionality of its products in the context of architecture and interior design for its presence at the 2016 Light + Building trade fair. In response to this brief, in-house designer Kristof Pycke created a booth that looked to evocatively demonstrate the brand's sophisticated and architectonic approach to light as the creator of space.

An array of rectilinear volumes varying in dimensions formed the abstract, modernist structure of the 306 m² stand. Together, these elements created a dynamic spatial experience of intersections, overlaps and recesses, resulting in a striking play of shadows when illuminated

by Kreon products. A solid ceiling running through the centre of the stand, along with an enclosing layering of walls, enhanced the immersive sense of space. At the same time, these partitions also served as displays for the company's collection, freeing the middle of each room for lounge and conferences areas.

The minimal black and white colour scheme established an elegant uniformity in the display. What is more, black manifested itself in different materials – carpet, rubber granule flooring, semi-transparent screens and oxide steel walls – aiding the exploration of the interaction between light and surface.

AJ WALL LAMP
Design: Arne Jacobsen

Martin Sølyst

Japanese paper art
helps **GAMFRATESI** bring out
light's spatial characteristics in an
Escher-esque stand design

MILAN — For Louis Poulsen at Salone del Mobile's Euroluce 2017, GamFratesi sought to capture the distinctly Scandinavian yet unconventional spirit of the fellow Copenhagen-based lighting company with an at once sharp and otherworldly design.

The display's white, smooth surfaces and sharp right angles suggested the clean and practical minimalism of Danish design. However, GamFratesi cited Japanese paper art as their main inspiration for a booth design that looked to emphasise the effects of cuts, lines and shapes on lighting. A Japanese maple tree at the entrance flanked by two of Louis Poulsen's PH Artichoke lamps made this homage explicit and set a serene mood for the exhibition.

Staircases protruded from the walls at different heights and orientations, in a surreal spectacle that recalled M C Escher's *Relativity* print and invited visitors to explore its every corner and side. Illuminated by Louis Poulsen's products from various directions, these angular forms created striking and dramatic shadows that gave the bare white structure a theatrical expression. By staging the brand's collection in abstract rather than realistic contexts, the designers conveyed the vast spectrum of potential ambiences that the products can create.

A surreal spectacle reminiscent of Escher's *Relativity* print invites visitors to explore the stand's every corner and side

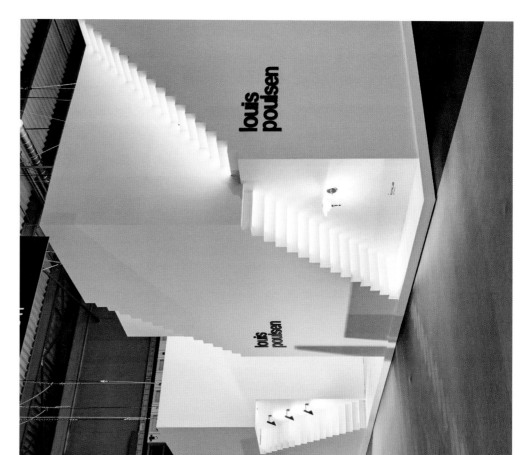

The stand challenged the boundary between interior and exterior, inviting exploration of each corner with displays of some of the company's products in the recesses created by the staircases outside.

E06

Collages of industrial materials by STEFANO COLLI define spaces for a lighting brand's collections

A translucent, rugged, imperfect skin of corrugated polycarbonate sheets is illuminated from the inside by Marset's products

MILAN — The collaboration between Barcelona decorative lamp manufacturer Marset and local design studio Stefano Colli spans over two decades. Like the offices, showrooms and past stands that Colli has designed for Marset, the atmosphere of the brand's presence at Salone del Mobile 2017 eschews sophistication and pretence for raw, untreated and often decontextualized materials in a continuously evolving concept. As the designer puts it, 'the Marset stand has become an evolutionary discourse.'

Various materials from the construction industry were used to define spaces for the brand's collections. The main frame of the exhibition comprised a visible orthogonal structure of natural pine slats that extended down to the floor along the interior to form rectilinear partitions. The construction materials were applied to the frame, forming a bare and unassuming container.

A translucent yet rugged and imperfect skin of corrugated polycarbonate cladded the exterior, illuminated from the inside by Marset's products. The interior walls and floors were finished with white-stained agglomerate, its opaqueness delimiting the spaces of service. Contrasting black materials ranging from polycarbonate and MDF boards to foam acoustic sheets formed distinctive and coherent backgrounds for the products. Sporadic use of packaging bubble wrap enriched the textural palette of the display.

Gathering spaces featured Luco stools by Martin Azua and Oxi Bistrot tables by JM Tremoleda and JM Massana, as well as antique Persian rugs.

SHAPE UP

A stand design by O/M LIGHT and **POR VOCAÇÃO** challenges visitors to conceive light as a creative primary material

O/M LIGHT

FRANKFURT — Clarity, quality, simplicity and consistency — these were the four key words that defined the briefing for O/M Light's stand at Light + Building 2016. The lighting company collaborated with fellow Porto-based creative marketing studio Por Vocação to create a brand narrative that sought to invert traditional preconceptions towards O/M's medium, emphasising light's sufficiency as an architectonic element. Atelier da Boavista, an architects' collective, also assisted in fine-tuning the spaces' proportions and lighting, as well as drafting plans.

Rather than creating spaces to be illuminated, the team began with light and used it to shape spaces. O/M's lighting products defined an area of abstract, geometric volumes, demonstrating the difference that refined control over optics and reflectors could make in construction. Intersections between the volumes formed entrances and passages, while light and darkness produced a stark (and somewhat antithetical) contrast between inside and outside. The exterior was clad in a monochrome black, whereas the interiors of the volumes were entirely white, with walls, floors and ceilings forming a single, continuous stage for precisely modulated plays of light and shadow.

Product information was displayed boldly and directly under each of O/M's luminaires, eliminating the need for secondary light sources. The stand design proved unique and memorable in that visitors could experience an architecture in which light was sincerely treated as a raw material.

Rather than creating interiors to be illuminated, the team begins with light and uses it to shape space

A sequence of radial phrases on the floor exemplified light as a primary material, in which mass — the round table — became an obstruction or complement to light, producing a shadow in the void within the words.

ROTO FRANK

ATELIER 522 builds a village for the display of door and window fittings

Benedikt Decker

Bright-red pendant lighting, whose minimalism mirrored the linear surfaces of the houses, illuminated the bar and informal meeting area.

NUREMBERG — German design firm atelier 522 marked its fourth collaboration with international manufacturer of window and door technology, Roto Frank, at the 2016 Fensterbau Frontale. Adopting 'stability connects', as its theme, the stand comprised a village of 21 houses that formed a fantastical setting in which visitors could discover and experience Roto's complete product line.

The houses were reduced to simple, archetypal shells, cast in a stark white with bright red pathways and accents that emulate the brand's image. While their open design pointed towards transparency as one of the company's key values, a more direct communication strategy consisted in guiding systems and visuals that allowed the brand to articulate its concepts with both detail and efficiency. What is more, by integrating Roto's products into the houses' fronts and interiors, the designers allowed visitors to experience them in a plausible setting.

Displays consisted of graphic elements illustrating technical and corporate data; tactile and interactive components, such as a hand-cranked sequence of gears that demonstrated the potential of Roto's products; and playful configurations, like a series of window handles hung together to form a large composite of themselves, or a plethora of door hinges arranged to form a labyrinth.

Lorenzo Pennati

ROYAL CERAMICA

PAOLO CESARETTI
conveys a fluid visual identity through a louvered façade

BOLOGNA — Florentine designer Paolo Cesaretti carries an intimate understanding of Royal Ceramica's multifaceted identity from his longstanding collaboration with the Egyptian tile maker. It is only natural, then, that he decided to incorporate this characteristic into the brand's presence at Cersaie 2014.

The stand comprised three rectangular volumes that were each clad in a triple-stained vertical brise soleil. As visitors moved around the space, the louvres morphed from red and purple to red and blue-grey, an optical effect that looked to mirror the brand's versatility through a fluid visual identity. The tripartite colour scheme foreshadowed the thematic division of the exhibition area inside. Royal Ceramica's diverse portfolio was in three different ways: hung like patterned fabrics, left leaning against easels like paintings, or covering the interiors of boxes like dramaturgical architecture.

In each case, the tile was conveyed as a fine work of art, displayed intimately in a compact and dense configuration. Their decorative qualities were enhanced by dynamic plays of light and shadow between the ambient illumination admitted through the exterior shade and theatrical lamps inside. After the exhibition area, a final, narrower volume served as a tranquil and secluded lounge for reflection and discussion.

Lorenzo Pennati

Stefano Stagni

Myriad collages of Royal Ceramica's tiles were displayed as works of art.

PAOLO CESARETTI finds decadence in detail with a secluded retreat for the display of ceramic panels

BOLOGNA — Hidden beneath an ornate veil, Egyptian company Royal Ceramica carried an exotic and mysterious presence at Cersaie 2015. The firm commissioned Paolo Cesaretti to construct a luxuriant environment that would give a comprehensive overview of the potential applications of its distinctive and multifarious product line.

A layer of MDF panels were suspended around the perimeter of a cantilevered,

rectangular roof. The panels were oriented vertically and horizontally, alternately overlaid, and perforated in a variety of elaborate patterns. Downlit and semi-transparent, they obscured the booth's interior, drawing visitors to discover what was inside.

On one side, framing the stand's reception, the panels receded upward to provide a generous and welcoming entrance. Upon crossing the threshold, one felt lost in the rich, geometric

silhouettes of the panels, which provided an immersive and meditative journey into abstractions of light and texture. Royal Ceramica's panels were displayed around a central cube in stylised, dynamic configurations. On the far end, clusters of bespoke furniture formed, along with the shading of the panels, a secluded retreat from the outside.

Ceramic panels were creatively displayed inside, angled weightlessly against each other or modulating in depth to create striking three dimensional effects, for example.

A comprehensive overview of the potential applications of the company's diverse line of ceramic panels

Stefano Stagni

SAMSUNG

ARIK LEVY's otherworldly, living sculpture embodies smart technology

BASEL — Samsung joined the international elite of watchmakers for the first time at Baselworld 2017 with an ambitious new smart watch line, the Gear S3. The South Korean conglomerate tapped internationally-renowned artist Arik Levy to design a radical architecture that would set the brand apart for its debut.

Inspired by his Rock series, Levy set out to create a 'living sculpture', a creature as conscious and interactive as the product's smart technology. A large shell comprising polygonal cells made of laminated, elastic material enclosed the longitudinal display area. Light from within gave the structure an ebullient, celestial glow, catching the fairgoer's eye from a distance. Entering the wide, jagged portal suggested boarding an alien vessel, its opaque facade giving no indication of what lay within.

No less perplexing than the outside, the interior imagined a remote location in space whose position and orientation could not be defined. Bright LED stripes interjected the white walls and ceiling at haphazard angles, enhancing the perspective of the room and making it appear to pulsate with life. Their motion was echoed softly in smooth, semi-reflective surfaces, resulting in a complex spatial dynamic. Opposite the product exhibits, a dark cinema area offered a 4D virtual reality experience of the Gear S3.

STUDIO DAVIDPOMPA

STUDIO DAVIDPOMPA demonstrates the design principles of its lighting products in an abstract collage

MEXICO CITY – Studio Davidpompa's lighting products are distinctive in their exploration of Mexican identity and the ways in which this character can be adapted to a simultaneous enthusiasm for modern and minimal forms. The studio's exhibition at the 2017 edition of Expo Lighting America turned this aspect of its aesthetic into a holistic architectural concept.

The stand consisted of overlapping walls in different colours and materials that together created a rich tonal collage. As opposed to defining a simple rectangular space, the partitions were asymmetrically placed, forming independent areas that allowed for free and open circulation. Raw metal surfaces and concrete

floors reflected the brand's affinity for honest materials and gave the atmosphere a sober and industrial character, while tropical plants injected a vitality and imagery characteristic of the Mexican landscape. Painted wooden surfaces paralleled this contrast: behind the black, white and greyscale hues of the reception area, a bright and festive pink was revealed.

Eschewing a ceiling altogether, the display instead implemented an exposed, modular metal structure, making the space appear more infinite and abstract. This framework served as a flexible support for the lamps, and the variety of colours and materials across the surfaces below helped bring out the qualities of each model.

The brand's Oola lamps were suspended haphazardly over a table that complemented their metallic materials.

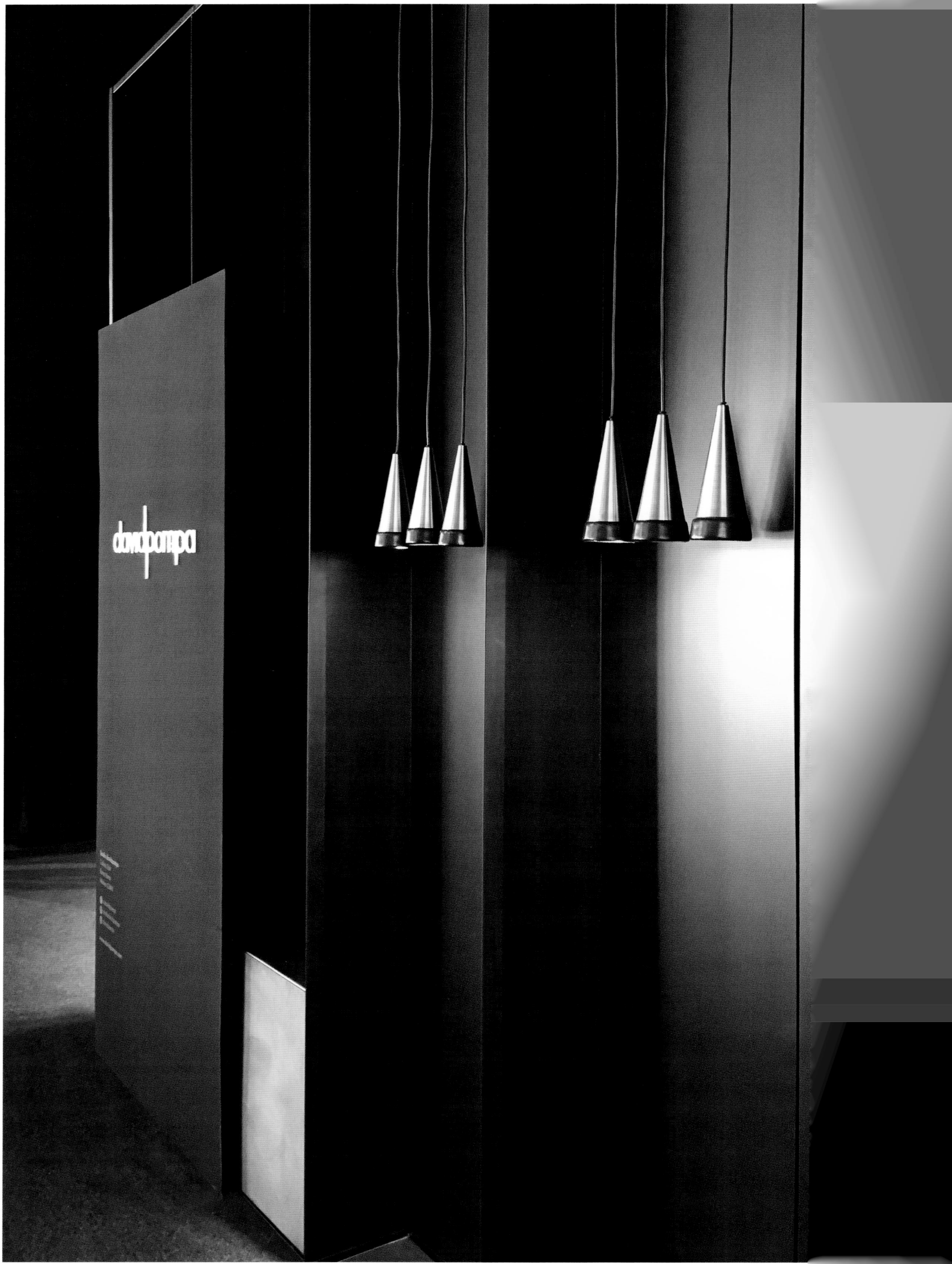
davidpompa

Asymmetrical partitions form independent areas that allow for free and open circulation

Caleta lamps hovered in a warm and lush atmosphere that highlighted their playful and organic qualities.

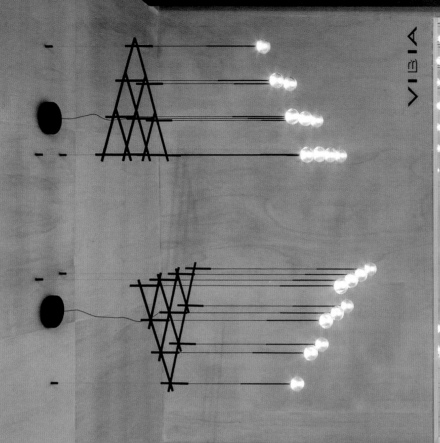

GRAND STAND 6

FRANCESC RIFÉ creates complex interactions between light and space through an architectural collage

Fernando Alda

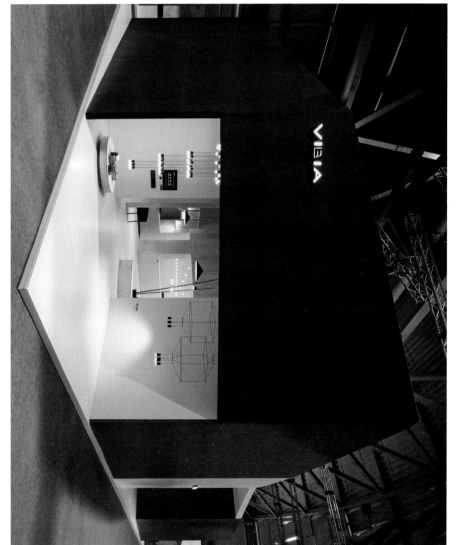

FRANKFURT – Catalonian designer Francesc Rifé continued his long-time collaboration with Barcelona lighting company Vibia in a striking, geometric stand design for Light + Building 2016. The miniature architectural space reproduced several building archetypes as a means of showcasing the versatility of the brand's products.

Two large, central masses displaying the company's latest products dominated the exhibition space, around which different architectural environments were arranged to form a continuous floor plan. Natural pine and poplar wood surfaces created a warm and organic contrast with the angular severity of the installation. Similar to previous editions,

elegant black interjected the wood tones and the company's signature whites and greys, while an additional rich blue, used to recall the brand's Mediterranean roots, brought a fresh element to the stand's architecture.

In a collage of flat, sloping, high and low spaces, Rifé explored each volume on its own and as part of an interconnected whole through the use of translucent fibres. These elements not only created a closer and more intercommunicative interaction between the spaces, allowing light to pass between them and thus establishing more complex lighting scenarios, but they also rendered certain volumes as 'lanterns' that allowed the spectator to perceive what was happening inside.

A reproduction of building archetypes is used as a means of showcasing the versatility of the brand's products

1   A translucent wall along the exterior incited fairgoers' curiosity as to what lay inside the stand.

2   Vibia's products were displayed against a variety of heights, shapes, colours, and materials, in order to fully demonstrate their potential.

SHOW

OFF

The stand as a stage

JEFFREY LUDLOW, Principal and Creative Director of 2×4 Madrid, considers how competition and constraints elevate the standards of stand design and the advantages of liberating the stand as a stage.

'You cannot hinge the success of a play solely on the set design'

Stand design is typically constrained by a tight budget and timeframe. How do you conciliate these restrictions with the need for innovative, eye-catching designs? Are these constraints an impediment on or fuel for creativity? Time and budget are indeed two big challenges. Even more so in stand design as you are creating a condensed version of a brand experience, or a concise way to communicate the brand. I think the first thing to do is to not see constraints and innovations on opposite sides. Time or budgetary restrictions help you to clarify the creative process, otherwise you could spin your wheels on deciding what shade of red is right. So I would say fuel.

What are the key factors that play into stand design? The first thing we do in this type of project is to make sure we understand the brand, in terms of tone, audience, ambitions, etc. Once we feel we have grasped that, we can begin to propose several ideas at once. Some ideas could be materially appealing, others more spatially focused and others still more visually interesting, through graphic applications, for example. The key factor is client dialogue as you begin to discover what the project wants to be.

The stand as a stage for the display of products is perhaps the most ubiquitous type of presence at trade fairs. Yet, this straightforward approach generates some of the most beautiful, eye-catching spaces. Why do you think that is? I think we have now become more and more locked into a calendar of global events. Fashion weeks, art fairs and design weeks, music/film festivals, etc. The booth, the pop up store and other types of ephemeral architecture have become a tool for brands to express themselves. With this came more competition within these architectural formats. So this has elevated the design of booths to become architectural follies more so then modular display methods.

How do you measure the success of a design? In the end the success of a booth depends more on when you as a designer have exited a project. In comes the real theatre of public interaction. We always plan for success, but there are some things you can't control and sometimes success, or lack thereof, comes down to logistics. In other words, you cannot hinge the success of a play solely on the set design.

What are the main advantages of this straightforward approach? The advantage of liberating the stand as a stage is that the main focus becomes the products and the narratives that they can create with lighting, colour, propping and styling. Architecture, which should maintain a subservient role in relation to the product, creates the structure for viewing and experiencing these interactions. If done well, you barely notice the mechanisms — or the magic — behind it.

How do you build engagement through this typology? The most interesting part of user engagement is how the booth, the brand and the products are shared via Instagram. It has become a way for a larger audience to see the booth even if they are not there. That will become, if it isn't already, the standard of engagement for booths. What a phone camera can frame is crucial to gaining more exposure to larger audiences. In our design for the Arper booth, for instance, we purposely designed the angles of each vignette as a way to increase the viewing area without limiting space.

How can these fleeting spaces make a lasting impact on a brand's image? The stand is one component of a larger brand universe that is part graphic, part digital, part advertising, part product. One thing we always want to make sure is to understand its role within the overall brand universe. You never want the booth to be the weakest link in communicating the brand. In our work for Arper, there is always a key theme or objective that we are trying to communicate and that is handed down to us. Whether it is play or colour, the booth is another expression of that theme in another format, so its lasting impact is its contribution to the larger brand conversations.

IS ESSENTIAL

COLOR

2X4 stages a simple brand narrative through a series of stripped-down, diorama-like scenes

ARPER

MATERIALS

CATIFA SENSIT

Angular sectors form individual displays whose vivid hues create popular photo-ops for visitors

MILAN — International design consultancy 2×4 continued its collaboration with Italian furniture company Arper in a booth design for the 2016 Salone del Mobile. From the outset, 2×4 had been charged with communicating Arper's core principles of simplicity, clarity and humanism in all of the brand's manifestations. The brief for this display, which celebrates a new line of the company's iconic Catifa chairs, opted for the same materials used in booths of prior years, but with a more internally-focused space.

The stand's structural elements consisted of rugged, honest materials such as lumber, scrim and plywood. Its entrance opened dramatically into a broad, circular room, with its edge divided into angular sectors that formed individual displays. Exposed pale timber and scrim partitioned these areas, making them appear as if they were dioramas. The semi-transparency of the scrim sustained an ambience of light and openness even in the enclosed, compartmentalised space. The predominant natural tone of the wood was interspersed with lively, vivid hues that accentuated the new colours available in the Catifa collection. Each scene's contents were organized in clear layouts that allowed for direct perspectives and deep focus. The result was an understated yet cogent brand narrative that became a popular Instagram photo-op for visitors.

1 Ceiling fixtures made of timber and scrim created visual continuity, both materially with the walls, and geometrically with the floor plan.

2 The 'stages' surrounded a central lounge area, where visitors could stop to take on the stand's relaxed atmosphere and experience some of Arper's pieces.

Gustav Karlsson Frost

JOHANNA MEYER– GROHBRÜGGE sets a playful, minimal stage for two new furniture collections

STOCKHOLM – Finnish furniture company Artek took over a space in the MDT dance theatre for Stockholm Design Week 2017, presenting two new collections of furniture and accessories by Norwegian designer Daniel Rybakken. The Berlin-based studio of Johanna Meyer-Grohbrügge realised the concept, inspired by the geometric eccentricity of one of Rybakken's products.

The brief required that each of the pieces be presented separately from each other and in an arrangement that reflected both artistic ingenuity and domestic realism. Derived from the 124 degree angle that defined Rybakken's mirror diptychs, a radial platform was split into three theatrical showrooms, each sparsely staged with a backdrop consisting of black-outline drawings onto a white background.

In one vignette, the dual mirrors of the 124° series hovered over an imaginary skyline, reflecting light in all directions. In another, a forested landscape accentuated the organic simplicity of the tripod-shaped coatracks and functionalist seats of the Kiila series. Finally, highlights from the two series were united in the minimalist dining room interior of a third vignette.

Each of the sections additionally served as a dynamic space for lectures and meetings as well as informal social gatherings. In line with the current programming of the MTD theatre, the exhibition aimed to serve as a stage that could be inhabited by visitors.

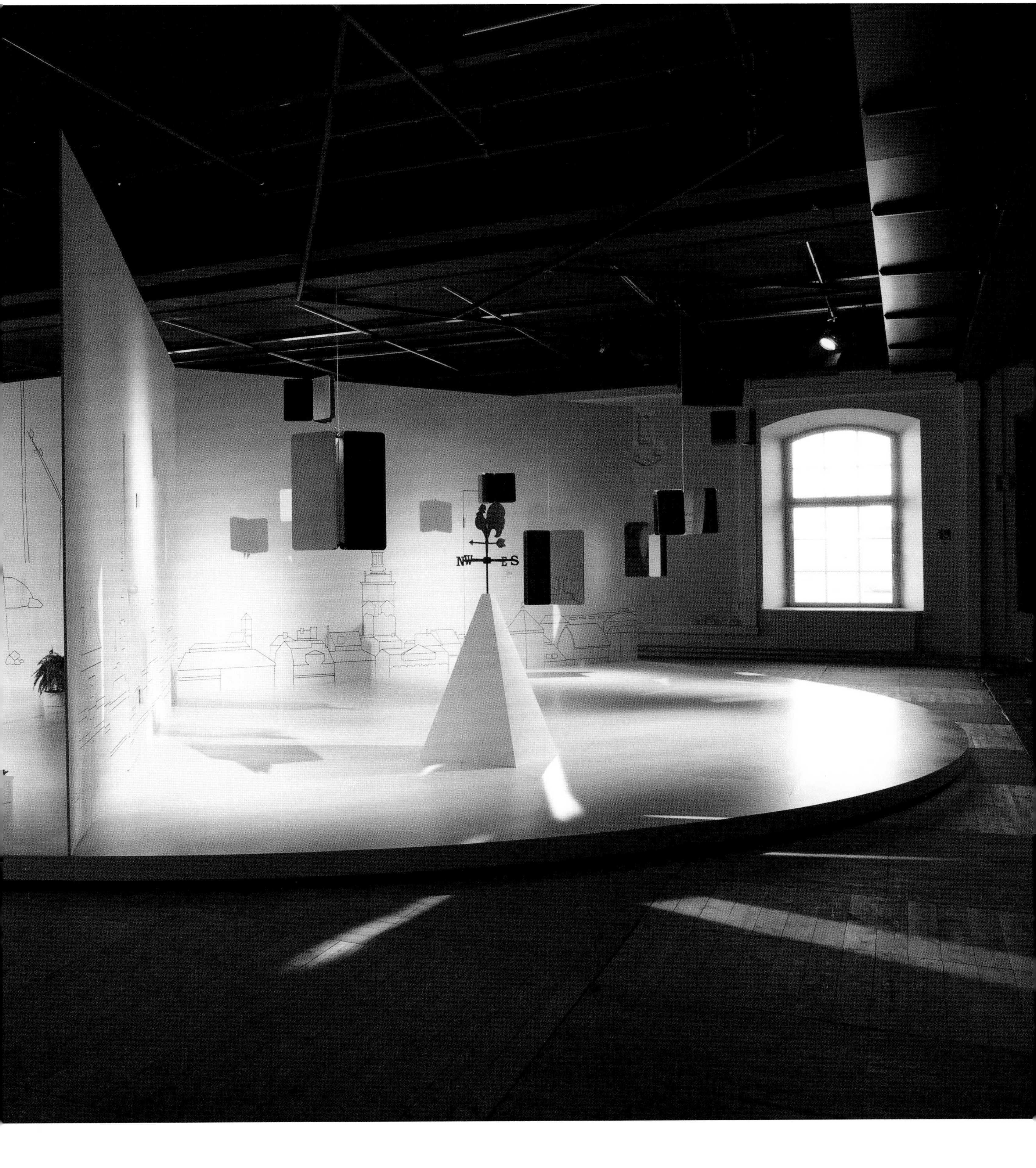

STEFANO COLLI and RAMÓN ÚBEDA create a holistic and theatrical spatial concept for a furniture brand's collections

MILAN — For a time, Barcelona furniture brand BD carried the slogan 'BD is not a style'. The company makes no pretences as to the eclecticism of its collections, the product of a wide and prestigious network of designers. While its variety of products share more general attributes like quality and craftsmanship, unifying them in a physical concept has always proved to be one of the brand's most significant challenges. What is more, working with the small exhibition spaces allotted to companies at trade fairs adds yet another hurdle to the process.

Designers Stefano Colli and Ramón Úbeda collaborated on the design concept for BD's presence at Salone del Mobile 2016, developing a stand that ensured the brand's characterful products at once stood out and coexisted harmoniously. Double-height wall flanking

two sides of the square slot were divided into several vignettes, each featuring products from a different collection. Solid colours or lightweight textiles served as backgrounds to these boxes, creating a vibrant and theatrical display that distinguished the collections without compromising a holistic sense of space.

Making the most use of the its corner location, the displays give a global vision of the company's products, appearing almost like two pages of an open comic book. The ceiling was deliberately left open so as not to make the modest, 100 m² exhibition area seem too confined. A simple black framework supported the lights in its stead. Colli and Úbeda's design was so successful that it has since been adapted to BD Barcelona Design's new collections presented at Salone del Mobile.

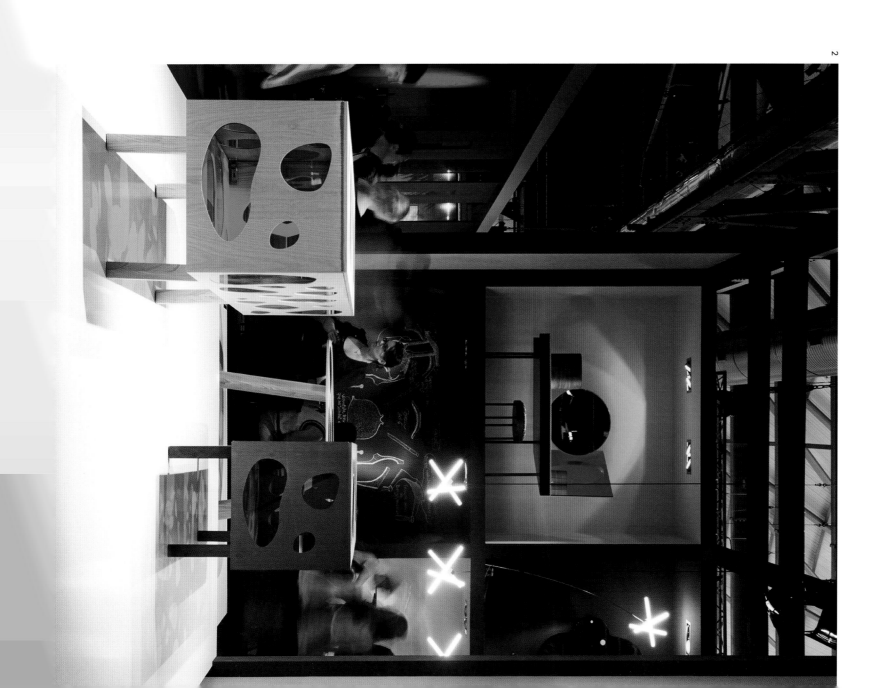

1

2

1 The ceiling was deliberately left open so as not to make the modest, 100 m² exhibition area seem too confined. A simple black framework supported the lights in its stead.

2 A central stage utilised tiered platforms to isolate highlight pieces, such as the Aquario cabinet and tables.

Daniel Schäfer

BRAAS

It took a village by UNIPLAN to display roofing solutions in a realistic and inviting setting

MUNICH – Building materials manufacturer Braas gave a comprehensive presentation of its latest system solutions for sloping roofs at BAU 2017 with a new booth design by Uniplan. The agency sought to make the company's presence more open, accessible and conspicuous to visitors, implementing a clear and congenial design that optimally showcased the products and promoted dialogue around them.

Offering a realistic demonstration of their aesthetic and functional features, the booth displayed the products on slanted surfaces of different sizes and angles. Together, these structures formed the roofs of the Braas Village, which was divided into two expansive product districts: tiles and slates. Visitors could walk through the cobblestone-print streets of this town and observe the roofing systems close up. A large, open area with a real tree at the centre of the exhibition served as the 'village square', a place where people could meet and exchange ideas.

Interactive elements enhanced the amiability and intrigue of the village. A climbing competition allowed visitors to test the safety and sturdiness of the product by scaling six metres up the facade of one of the village 'houses'.

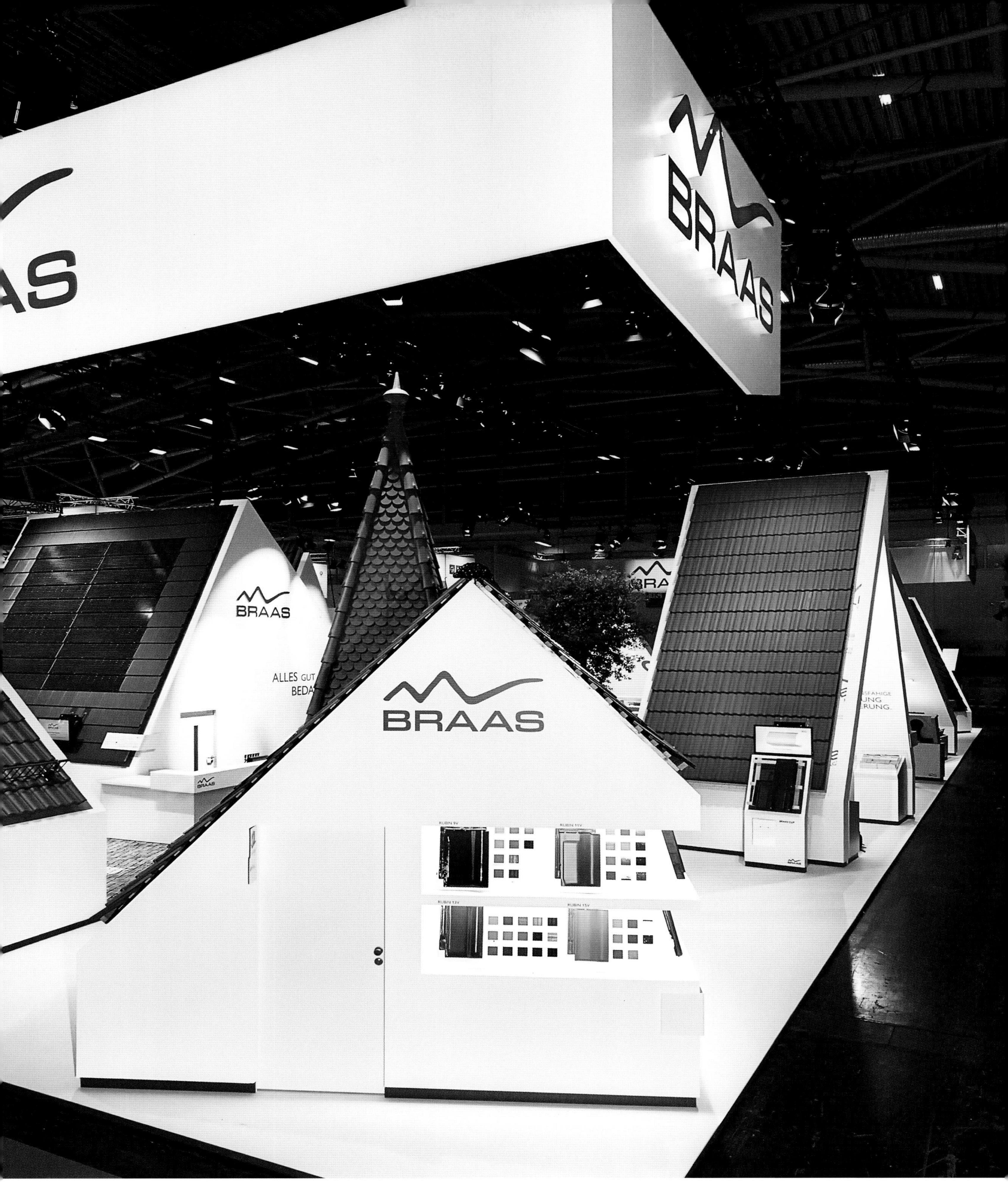
BRAAS
BRAAS
BRAAS
ALLES GUT
BEDA

Design is
a state
of matter

Design is
a state
of matter

009

ALESSANDRA DALLOLI communicates
the beauty of technical rigour in a
minimalist stand recalling museum exhibits

1

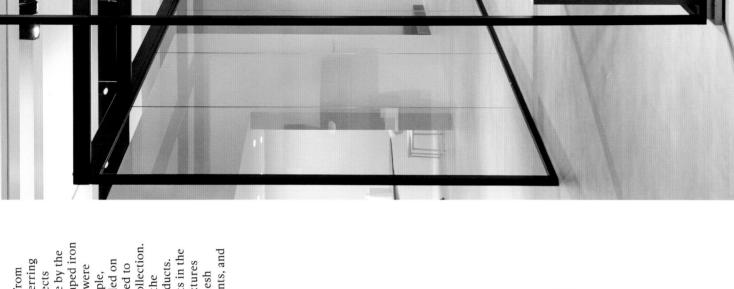

MILAN — For its presence at the 2017 Salone del Mobile, Desalto wanted to convey its half-century tradition of close unity between aesthetic refinement and technical research. The Italian furniture brand commissioned architect Alessandra Dalloli to present its new collection, whose renewal and transformation lies in a 'metamorphosis' of materials, by incorporating the stand concept into the new catalogue's overarching narrative. The result was an open, sophisticated design that resembled a museum display.

Sitting in a corner slot, the installation consisted of a neutral, warm grey box with two open fronts revealing the exhibition inside. Products were placed in two types of minimalist display cases. The first was a large box whose pale pink glass walls were constructed from out of production materials, thus transferring a sense of rarity and treasure to the objects inside. The second type of cases — made by the company itself from trims of square-shaped iron tubing used in its Helsinki collection — were placed around the central box. The simple, black rectangles could be easily assembled on site thanks to the use of joints, and served to objectively frame key pieces from the collection.

Much like in a museum, light was the key player in emphasising Desalto's products. Concentric bands illuminated the objects in the display cases, while controlled-beam fixtures were mounted strategically in a white mesh spanning the ceiling to create both accents, and a sense of transparency in the space.

Like in a museum, light is the key player in emphasising Desalto's products

1 The stand reflected a desire to create an understated space with a sensibility for classical proportions.

2 Graphic and textual elements on the walls provided information about the products in the context of the theme of transformation and metamorphosis.

DIMORESTUDIO's decadent garden pavilion explores the boundaries between indoor and outdoor

BASEL — For the 2016 edition of Design Miami/Basel's Design at Large series, studios were invited to go beyond the constraints of a conventional booth and explore the theme of Landscape in immersive, large-scale installations. Inspired by Italian gardens of the early and mid-twentieth century, Milanese firm Dimore Studio constructed Verande, a lush pavilion that served as a proposition for a place inhabiting both indoor and outdoor space.

A canopy was supported by interior columns placed away from the pavilion's edges, so that this mass and the curtains that hung from it appeared to hover weightlessly in the fair. Its exterior cladding of deep red beaded wood contrasted with the sheer, light blue cotton curtains, gently rustled by ceiling fans inside, as if caught in a breeze. Upon entering, visitors were enveloped in a verdant arrangement of tropical plants. A geometric design comprising black and grey bands growing seamlessly from the floor up the columns and along the perimeter of the ceiling was set against marble-effect linoleum, serving as an abstract complement to the wild, organic quality of this jungle-like garden.

Furniture evocative of mid-century modern icons accentuated the romantic aspect of the space with a colour scheme of reds, creams, white and navy blues, alongside brass detailing. In its languid depiction of a bygone era, Verande invited visitors to relax in a removed setting where time stood still.

1 Britt Moran and Emiliano Salci's outdoors furniture collection adorned the pavilion.

2 Coming from the ceiling fans, a gentle breeze rustled through the pavilion's exotic plants, creating a lush garden effect.

RAUMKONTOR promotes the expressive freedom of wallpaper with a cabinet of curiosities

Hans Juergen Landes

COLOGNE – Raumkontor readily admits that complexity always underlies even the simplest and most minimal designs – it is simply the consequence of living in a highly complex world. The Dusseldorf-based agency explored this concept at its logical extreme in a booth design at the 2016 IMM Cologne for the German wallpaper trade association Deutsches Tapeten-Institut.

Four compartments were carved out of a black, rectangular two-level volume. Each compartment hosted a room with a different monochromatic colour scheme set by a vibrant wallpaper. The interiors were cluttered with eclectic arrays of furniture, objects, trash and pop culture ephemera – forming a modern cabinet of curiosities.

Departing from the notion that the product is the main event of the trade fair booth, the exhibition allowed each of its rooms to become an event in itself, promoting the idea that wallpaper allows one the freedom to express feelings and develop their personality. At the same time, as an artistic photo-op, the dense and varied backdrops of the display provided a space for visitors to create their own social narratives, exemplifying media-effective communication.

1 Capitalising on the idea of the stand as an event, playful live acts staged at particular times featured different characters interacting with each room, such as a dog.

As an artistic photo op, the dense and varied backdrops provide a space for visitors to create their own social narratives

DURSTONE

VXLAB
unites two
distinct brand
voices with
a dynamic
spatial
experience
and a touch
of home

VALENCIA — VXLab collaborated once again with Spanish ceramic tile maker Durstone on a booth design for Cevisama 2017. The studio faced the same challenge as in the prior year, which was to create a cohesive space that would showcase the main product line as well as the company's signature Q collection, focusing on youthful and eclectic contemporary styles.

A black radial volume was embedded within a white rectilinear structure, the void between them serving as a corridor that ushered visitors inside. Inside the first, VXLab reprised its 'Blooming Gallery' concept to display the latest wares of the Q line. Conceived as an intimate cabin, this space primarily employed three raw materials for its surfaces and fixtures: pine, fabric and copper. These, along with a central planter, formed an ecological and understated backdrop for the tiles.

Moving out into the second structure, one encountered a more spacious recess cast in a nearly monochrome white with subtle black accents, opening up to the fair on one side like a modern and elegant loggia. This space conveyed the characteristic minimalism found in the products displayed along walls perpendicular to the opening, this way creating unique architectural perspectives when viewed from the outside.

1 Wooden alcoves were carved throughout the exterior of the radial wall to create small niches for private meetings.

2 In the Q area, the radial design is reflected from the ceiling to the floor, giving centre-stage to a meeting zone.

Filip Wolak

FERRUCCIO LAVIANI reflects a lighting brand's fresh perspective on its designs with a classic optical illusion

NEW YORK — 'To create something from nothing is itself an illusion; to give it volume, to make it physical, is an illusion,' says designer Ferruccio Laviani in reference to his work for Foscarini at New York Design Week 2016. The installation, which took place in Foscarini Spazio Soho, the brand's New York showroom, challenged visitors with one of the most essential philosophical questions: what is reality, and what is illusion?

The narrow, polygonal space of the exhibit was styled after a classic optical illusion known as the Ames room, in which objects appear larger or smaller than their actual size when viewed from a certain vantage point. As visitors moved deeper into the room, those standing at the threshold could observe the brand's large-scale versions of its classic designs appearing to expand and contract in size due to subtle inclines in the floor and walls. The unevenness of the surfaces was masked by a multi-coloured triangle pattern that covered the entire interior. The existing columns of the shop interior penetrated the enclosure, creating a false orthogonal perspective while establishing a sober contrast to the vibrant print. Foscarini's renditions, in 'L' and 'XL' versions, were dispersed throughout the room for visitors to discover, adding to the disorienting sense of proportion.

FERRUCCIO LAVIANI staggers disjointed partitions across a wide exhibition space to create a distinctive, layered display

Foscarini Spa

GRAND STAND 6

SHANGHAI – Ferruccio Laviani had to work with cumbersome dimensions for the Foscarini stand at the Salone del Mobile Milano/Shanghai 2017. The space was unusually wide and shallow, leading the designer's initial brainstorming to conjure up a tunnel installation, similar to what he had done with previous works for the Italian lighting company. The resulting stand took a much different course, placing primary emphasis on the façade over the pathway.

The structure consisted of disjointed partitions parallel to the plane of the entrance that together formed a sequence of 'layers'. These partitions were cast almost entirely in a bright red for maximum visibility and impact, with the Foscarini logo, deconstructed in large white letters across the three frontmost partitions, being the only exception to the monochrome colour scheme of this bold and distinctive façade. Concentric circles were punched through

each of the partitions to form telescoping windows into the exhibition space. The punctures playfully revealed Foscarini's products placed within the layers and allowed them to interact with each other both horizontally and vertically. Visitors could glance into the booth, meander through the layers, and lookout onto the hallway, creating a complex architectural and social theatre.

Laviani took inspiration for the telescoping punctures from the opening credits in the James Bond film *GoldenEye*.

Punctures in the partitions playfully reveal Foscarini's products in a complex architectural and social theatre

COLOGNE — The ability to adapt to an ever-changing and unpredictable market has become an almost universal theme in contemporary brand messaging. Even though one might not immediately consider this notion in the context of the furniture market, which is rooted to a certain extent in timeless classics, hülsta commissioned Triad Berlin to portray the company as an innovative pioneer navigating the protean course of the industry.

For hülsta's booth at the 2016 IMM Cologne, the Berlin-based design agency developed a kinetic sculpture comprising nearly 8 km of rope that spanned the exhibition area. Its individual strands were oriented vertically and parallel to each other along small rails that were allowed

a range of free movement. The ambient air circulation of the room kept the installation in constant motion, creating a changing sequence of perspectives and spatial impressions and establishing a serene connection with the surrounding environment.

The sculpture formed natural partitions for the stand's four distinct living areas, while lending the space a sense of openness and transparency. Experiencing hülsta's products in such abstracted living spaces allowed one to conjure a diverse array of possible interiors to which they could be applied, thus serving as a compelling statement to the brand's dynamic character.

GRAND STAND 6

1 Neutral whites formed the colour scheme for the structural elements and the rope installation, shifting emphasis on its motion and perspective, as well as the available colours of the furniture.

2 Low, geometric partitions divided the 950 m² stand into diverse interior settings.

Ulf Bueschieb

HÜLSTA

A kinetic sculpture by **TRIAD BERLIN** communicates a furniture brand's dynamic character and innovative force in a changing market

2

The stand included products produced by
Saphir Keramik and designed by Toan Nguyen,
Konstantin Grcic, Stefano Giovannini and
Ludovica and Roberto Palomba.

Eleonora Rapacchietta

LAUFEN BATHROOMS

PALOMBA SERAFINI ASSOCIATI
draws a three-dimensional plan
of the bathroom of the future

A large mirror ceiling reveals the interiors as if abstract floor plans

COLOGNE — Swiss bathroom specialist Laufen was invited by Vitra to participate in its Work showcase at Orgatec 2016, an exploration of the future of work environments and the companies that will shape them. The century-old brand of high-end, complete bathroom solutions commissioned Milan studio Palomba Serafini Associati to assist in articulating a response to what modern sanitary rooms might look like in this context.

Five sleek, white volumes rose seamlessly from a platform, forming a facade of unassuming, geometric enigma. The boxes' contents would not be visible to passers-by if it wasn't for a large

mirror ceiling angled above them, revealing the interiors as if abstract floor plans. The company's products, spanning a variety of different utilities, filled these interiors, creating an individual design language in each that was accentuated by solid, bright floor finishes.

Emotively symbolising a sketch of the future from afar, these images could become concrete if one approached the stand to peer inside the boxes. More than an allegory, this display also served a practical function of allowing visitors to view Laufen's proposals for the modern sanitary room as both spatially closed and realistically scaled units.

Luke Hayes

A sophisticated merry-go-round reimagines iconic pieces spanning LEE BROOM's decade-long portfolio

MILAN — To commemorate his studio's tenth anniversary, Lee Broom was invited to create a portfolio-spanning exhibition for the 2017 Salone del Mobile. The display, entitled Time Machine, was no ordinary retrospective as the renowned British designer chose to reimagine his works in an entirely new material finish for a limited edition collection rather than displaying them in their original and iconic forms.

Set inside a disused vault at the Milano Centrale station, the stand glowed hauntingly in the form of a minimalist fairground carousel. The mechanism was a subject that had fascinated Broom since his childhood and which he often found himself sketching. In the context of the exhibit, its slow rotation offered a poetic and theatrical means of engaging with the designer's body of work through the metaphor of a lifecycle.

On the carousel's floor, pieces from Broom's furniture, lighting and accessories were found cast in a pristine white. Reduced to a single colour, the products took on a minimalist, modern semblance that emphasised their silhouette. Amongst these reinvented items, an elegant and monolithic grandfather clock in Carrara marble with brass pendulum, weights and hands — an exclusive design for the Time Machine collection — epitomised the spirit of the exhibition.

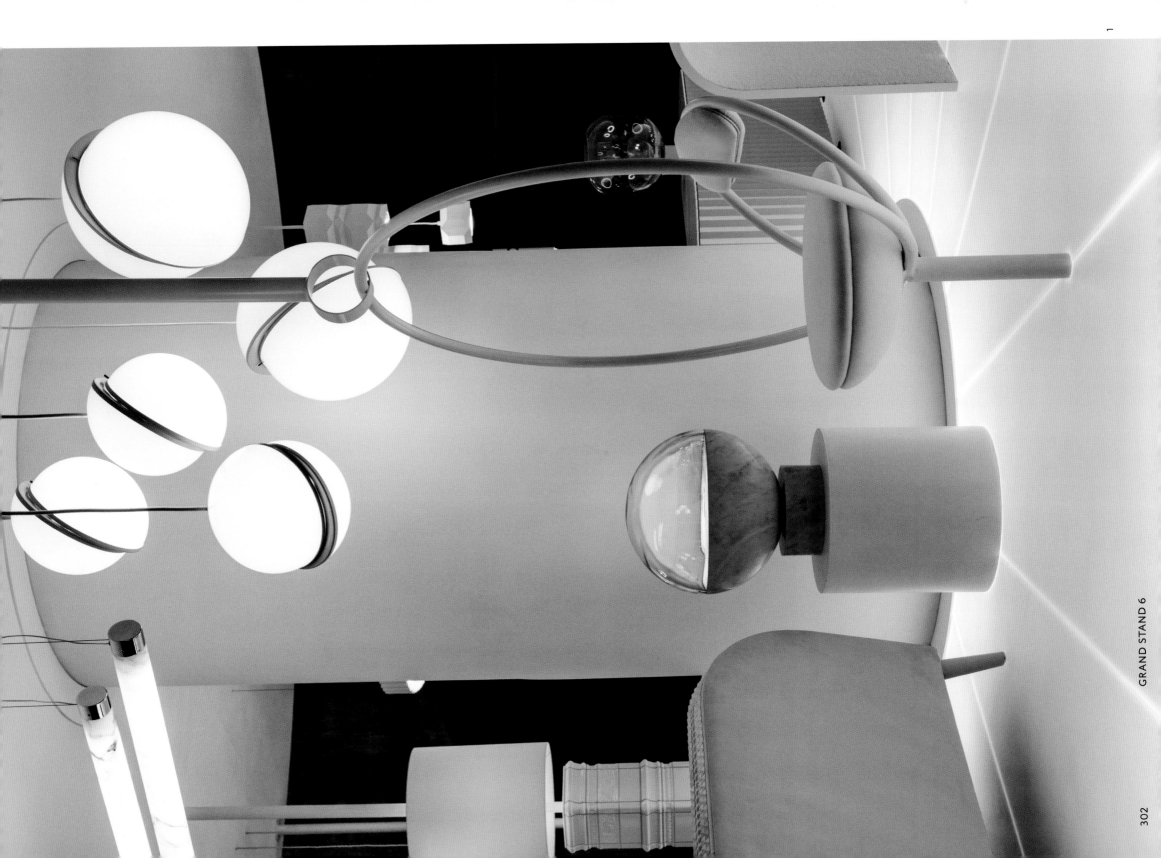

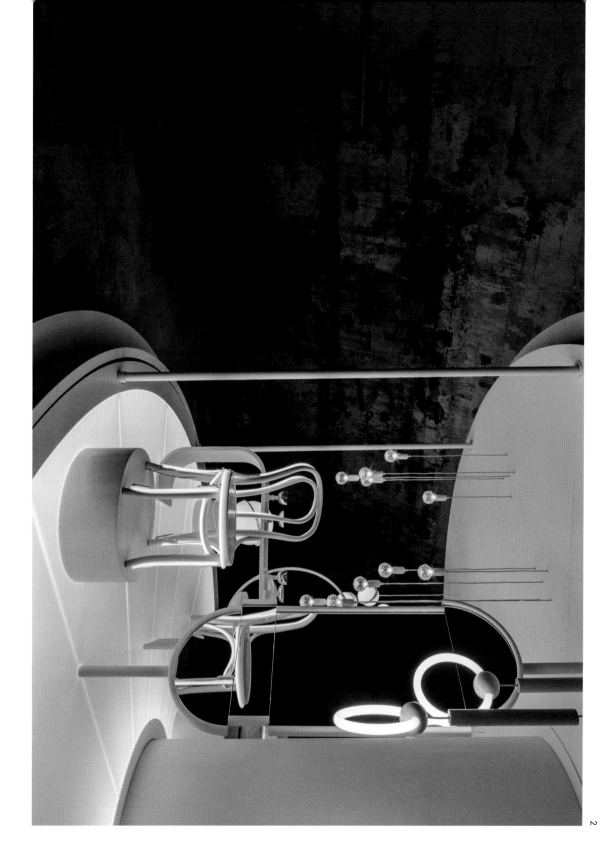

The carousel's slow rotation offers a poetic and theatrical means of engaging Broom's work through the metaphor of a lifecycle

1 Standing at over 6-m-wide and 4-m-high, the carousel was built in the famous Pinewood film studios in the UK.

2 Lit from beneath with LED panelling, the display was reminiscent of director Stanley Kubrick's film set designs.

NEMO

STUDIO VALENTINA FOLLI

creates a raw, industrial presence for a wide range of lighting products

FRANKFURT — Nemo had shied away from the spotlight for several years at Light + Building, so the company needed to make a strong and lasting impact for its return to the fair in 2016. Designer Valentina Folli's proposal for the stand was to showcase a wide range of new products while conveying their individual power and features to the fair's industry-based audience.

Inspired by the light, fresh and dynamic character of the company, Folli implemented a clean and streamlined colour and material vocabulary in her concept. A C-shaped wall structure made from recycled industrial scaffolding formed a 'lighting fort' and was framed by a 5-m-high coated MDF wall with the Nemo logo. The flexibility of the fort supported custom installations for each product, with functional use of perforated metal sheets for some of the more slender designs.

The floor was formed from industrial aluminium sheets that reflected and accentuated the products' light. Toward the back of the exhibition space, an 8-m-long counter was illuminated by one of Nemo's most distinctive products for that year, a minimal, modular lighting system consisting of LED profiles. The raw and stripped-down design fostered an atmosphere in which the products became the main attraction.

The stand's scaffolding structure featured powder coating finishes that accentuated the industrial aesthetic and created a uniform grey tonality.

Folli's stripped-down design fosters
an atmosphere in which the products
become the main attraction

NORMANN COPENHAGEN
promotes its in-house collection with a series of elegant tonal universes

Normann Copenhagen

Different upholstery options for the Ace chair placed side by side demonstrated the versatility of the design.

MILAN – Hans Hornemann was the star of Normann Copenhagen's exhibition at the 2016 Salone del Mobile. The in-house designer for the Danish furniture brand presented his new collection, Ace, which combines urban lifestyle and luxurious upholstery with functional, flat-pack principles. Hornemann himself conceived the display for his designs: a series of tonal universes inspired in the colour choices for the new product line.

Introducing visitors first to the shapes and contours of the furniture pieces, the front area of the booth made predominant use of a light, neutral beige colour. In this section, rich, thick carpets

created a lush and warm atmosphere, while raised podiums allowed highlight pieces to be viewed from different angles. Farther back into the display, these carpets took on vivid monochrome hues that set the tone for different sceneries, each divided by translucent partitions in bright colours that allowed one to catch a glimpse of adjacent areas.

At the centre of the booth, clear acrylic boxes visualised the flat-pack feature of the collection by displaying components of disassembled Ace chairs. A contrasting mix of polished and brushed steel surfaces along the back of the exhibition disguised the stand's storage space by mirroring its diverse range of colours.

PEDRALI

A collection of corporate furniture finds an unlikely identity in CALVI BRAMBILLA's ironic office

COLOGNE — At Orgatec 2016, Milanese studio Calvi Brambilla presented Pedrali's new collection of office furniture with a light-hearted, tongue-in-cheek design. The appeal of the colourful, 370 m² stand lay more in the subtle uncanniness of the different displays than in its grand scale or holistic spectacle.

Two trapezoidal blocks defined the boundaries of the exhibition, the spatial enigma of its receding entrance beckoning the visitor inside. Four cubic recesses of varying dimensions were carved into each block and functioned as showrooms for each of the products. The

linearity of the structure harmonised with the design of the Pedrali furniture, while the vibrant surfaces of the alcoves complemented or else formed direct counterpoints to the furniture's minimalistic lines.

Upon glancing into the dollhouse-like vignettes, the visitor discovered touches of playful surrealism, such as a shark swimming in a window of a waiting room or paper boats sailing on a conference table. The interjection of these dreamlike elements created an arresting and provocative dialogue with the corporate context of the furniture.

Touches of playful surrealism adorn the stand's dollhouse-like vignettes

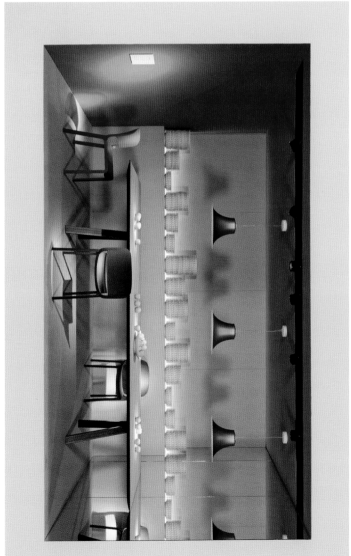

All firmly connected to the workspace, different settings portrayed in eight alcoves included a meeting room, a waiting room, and a company restaurant.

Pierre Charpin

PIERRE CHARPIN designs a retrospective of his work that achieves visual impact with stark simplicity

PARIS — Designer, artist and scenographer Pierre Charpin was elected Designer of the Year for SAFI Salons' annual event Maison & Objet Paris in 2017. In this context, Charpin was granted a space at the fair in which he could showcase the diversity of his portfolio. Beyond unifying works from disparate fields into a coherent concept, his challenge for the stand was to create a display that would read as an exhibition space as opposed to a commercial space.

Using the stand's location in the corner of the exhibition hall to his advantage, Charpin organised his pieces in a way that allowed them to be discovered progressively as one moved around the rectilinear space. The works rested on a minimal, white platform that appeared like an island against the black surfaces of the hall. Four doubled-sided partitions were placed at staggered intervals and framed the stand's remaining objects.

On the front side of each partition, an iconic motif from Charpin's formal language, the geometric 'formes noires', established a strong visual impact commensurate with the scale of the room. A carefully curated selection of works around these monoliths followed a principle of separation by stark simplicity, displayed without platform or pretension, sparingly placed so as to allow the space to breathe.

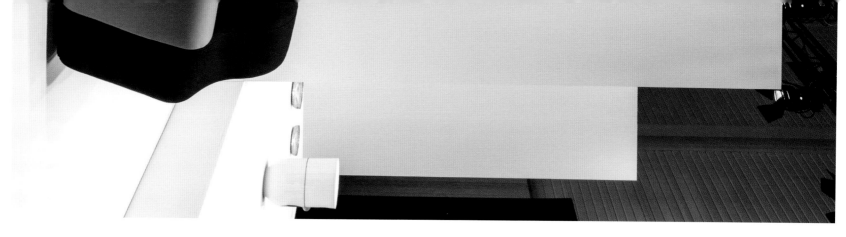

Along the back of one of the partitions, eight LED screens formed an animated display that provided further insight into the designer's work.

Works can be discovered progressively, as visitors move around the rectilinear space

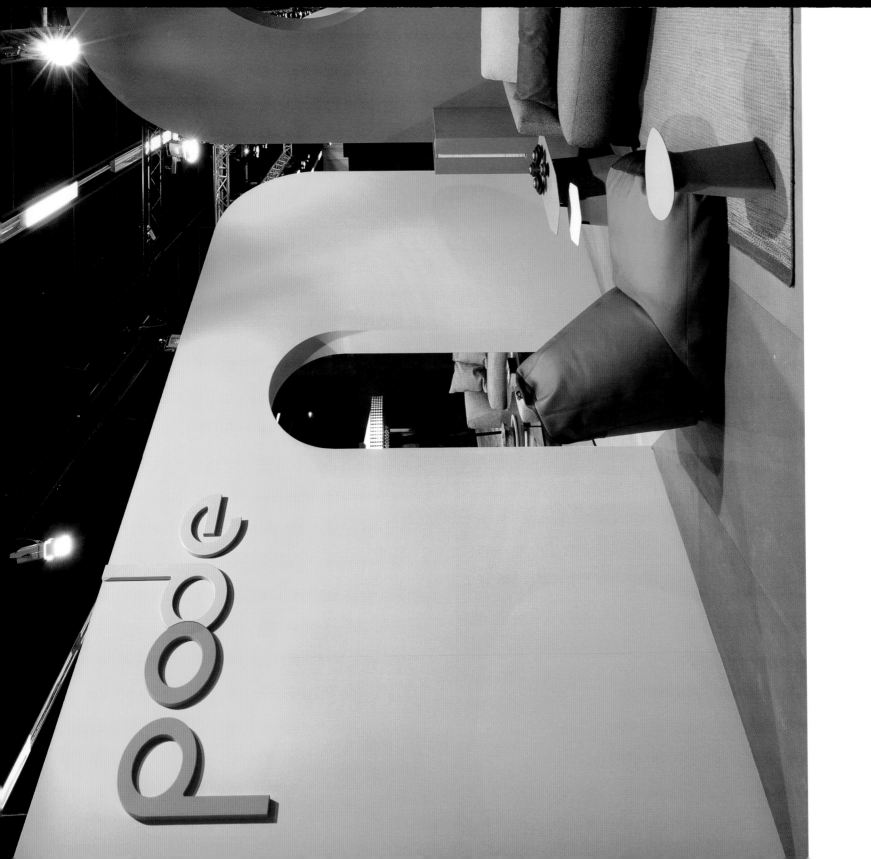

STUDIO RODERICK VOS turns a small floor plan into an intricate set of staged interiors

COLOGNE – Studio Roderick Vos stepped up as the new art director of Pode just in time to give the Dutch furniture brand (formerly specialising in seating) a makeover for its inaugural lifestyle collection. The latest incarnation of the Leolux sub-label debuted at IMM Cologne 2017, with the Claire and Roderick Vos's compact but vibrant booth design showcasing the brand's capability of creating a truly comprehensive and unique identity for an interior.

The main challenge for the stand was the need to formulate a cohesive display for a diverse and sizable product line on just a 9 × 9 m footprint. To optimise the lack of space without creating

visual chaos, the floor plan was partitioned into four distinct stages, alternating between living and dining areas. An accompanying magazine placed the furniture pieces in context and thus freed the space of information clutter.

The dividing walls varied in height and shape, and were each placed at a 35-degree angle from a strict grid to produce unique architectural views from each vantage point. The explosion of colour and texture in each room, combined with simple, geometric voids for doors and windows, presented a fresh take on the Memphis renaissance in contemporary interior design.

1   The partitions' different heights created an
    intimate atmosphere in each setting and made
    for an attractive overarching stand design.

2   Oversized coffers lining the walls of certain
    'rooms' enriched the display's textural and
    geometric palette.

An explosion of colour and texture combined with geometric voids presents a fresh take on the Memphis renaissance in contemporary interior design

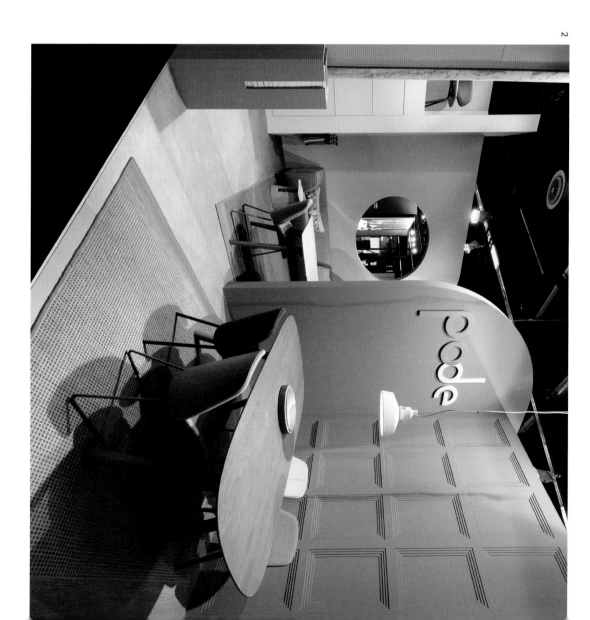

PRESSALIT

JYSK DISPLAY creates a stand that at once embraces and emphasises the products on display

GRAND STAND 6

322

FRANKFURT — 'We support you' was the message that Pressalit looked to convey at ISH 2017. Looking for a warm, inviting and distinctly Scandinavian presentation for its product line, the Danish bathroom equipment company hired design studio Jysk Display to create a new concept for their stand. The main requirements were 'a clear link in the shapes and colours used throughout the stand, [and] a perfect flow from one product group to another,' the designers explain.

A square plinth of raised, laminate flooring served as the base of the booth, from which a curved partition rose between the main information area and more secluded exhibition and meeting spaces. This screen of vertical, birch plywood slats and painted MDF panels also functioned as the backdrop for the display of the brand's wide range of items.

Openings in the curved wall gave passers-by a glimpse of the bar and meeting area beyond, to incite their curiosity. This secluded area provided a more intimate atmosphere for the display of some product groups, while the town square-inspired lobby featured a spiral reception desk and a tree, adding to the stand's organic design. Both the materials chosen and the stand's organic shapes contributed to an atmosphere of warmth and courtesy, the key words of the design concept.

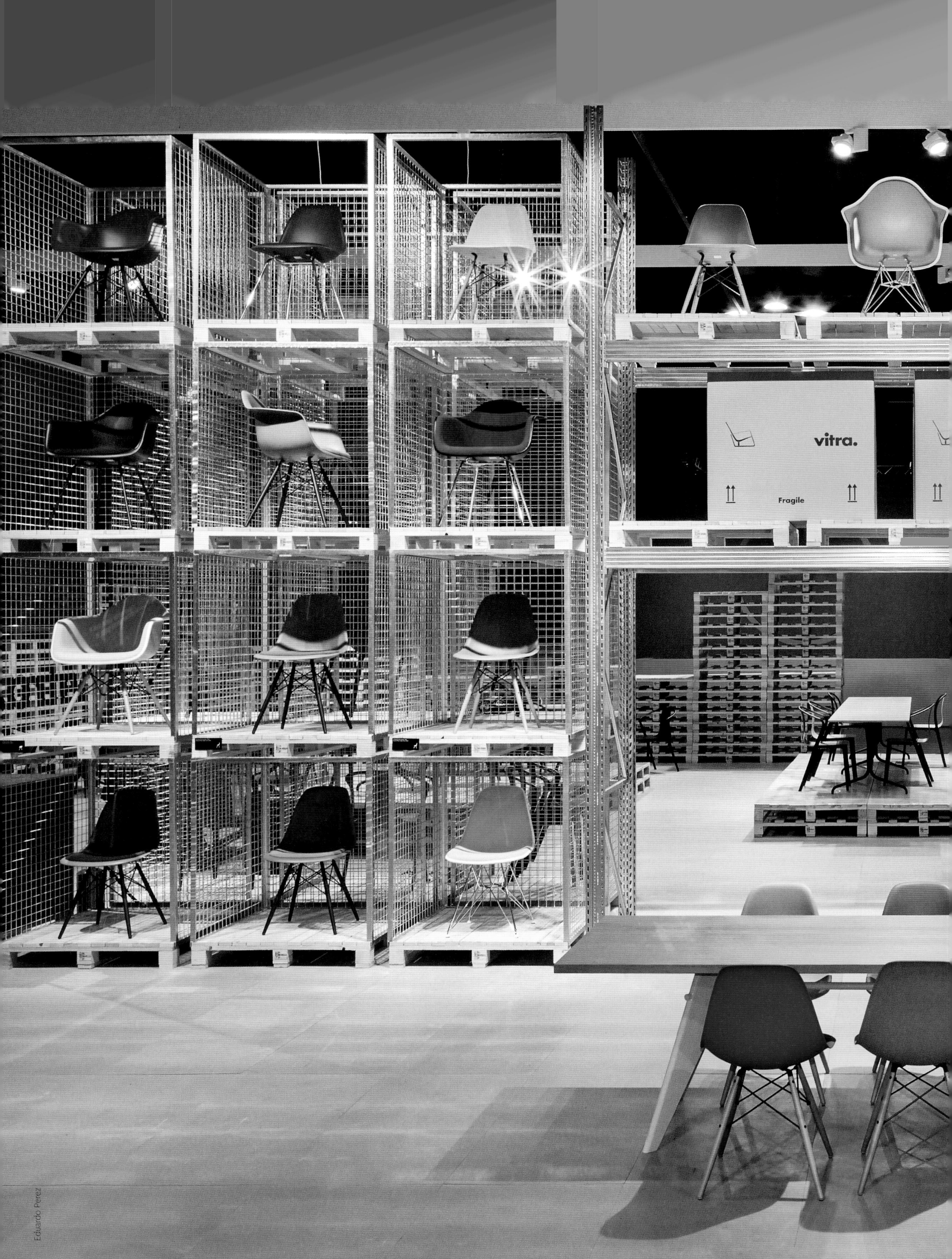

Eduardo Perez

VITRA

SCHEMATA puts up
a modular, industrial exhibition space for iconic furniture designs

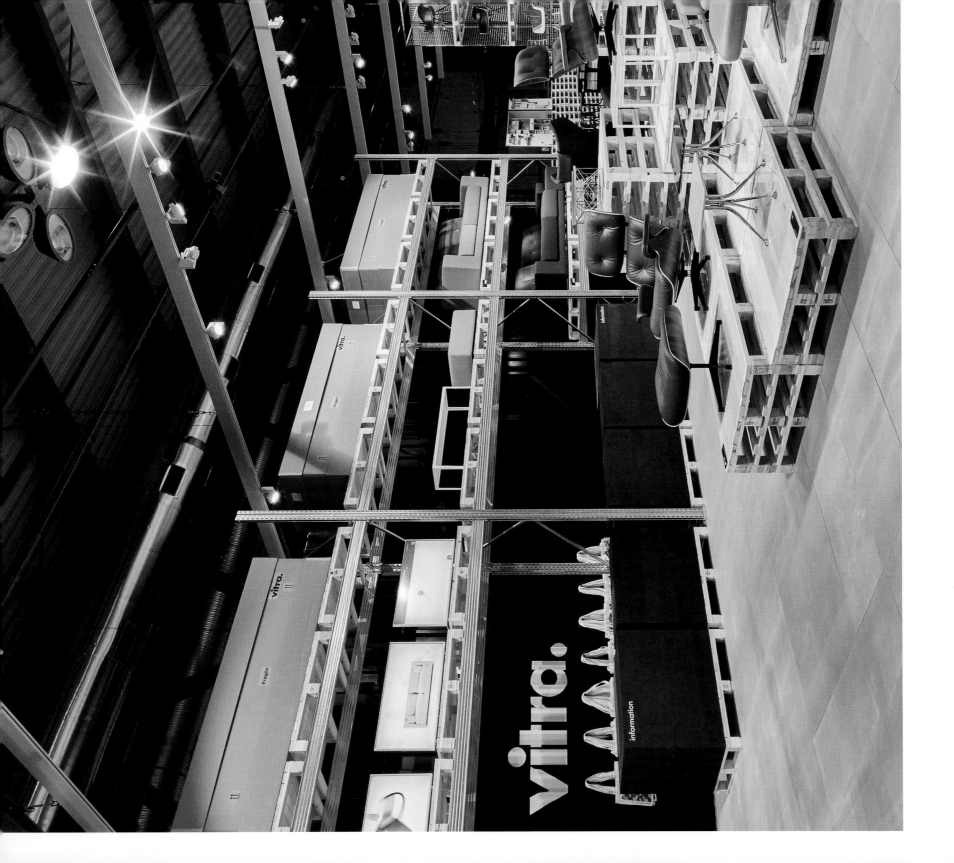

A DIY approach to the stand set up encourages the designers of each product to experiment with the 1 × 1 m modules

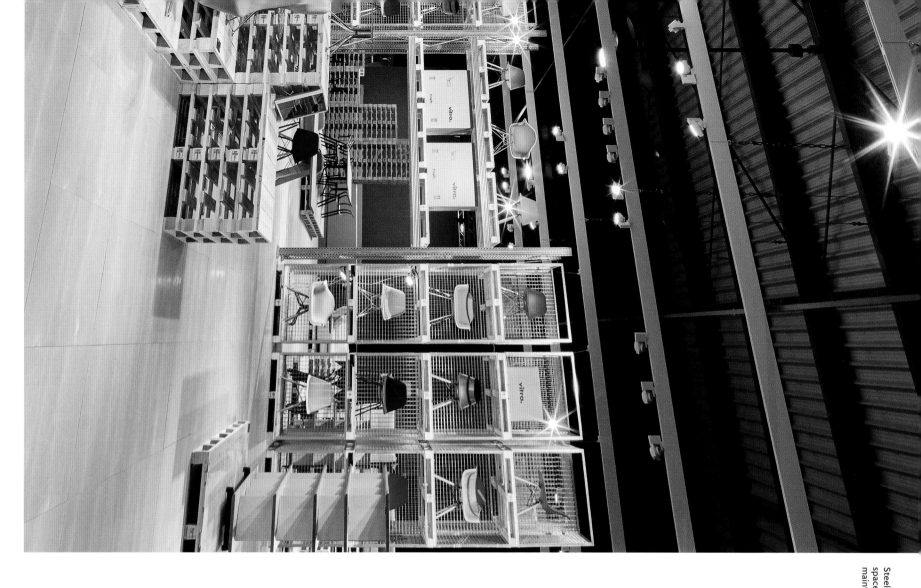

MILAN – For Vitra's presence at Salone del Mobile 2015, Tokyo-based studio Schemata sought to create a uniform and modular vocabulary that held infinite possibilities as both a display interface for the brand's designers and a spatial experience for the stand's visitors. Headed by Jo Nagasaka, the design firm departed from an idea of repetition inspired in Vitra's collection to develop an holistic stand concept.

Wooden pallets were stacked to form walls and platforms with varying heights. Refusing to impose any sense of orientation or boundary upon the visitor, the stand opted for an open-plan space styled after a piazza as opposed to a neutral white cube or secluded enclosure. This way, the exhibition allowed each viewer to choose their own approach to the stand and thus, to the products on display.

The pallets were based on a standard, 1 × 1 m model used in Japanese storage and shipping systems and could thus form flexible layouts for the display. Schemata adopted a DIY approach for the realisation, encouraging the designers of each furniture piece to experiment with the pallets as a means of discovering the optimal way to display the product. An epoxy resin finish spruced up the industrial rawness of the atmosphere and unified the free-form arrangement of the display.

Steel rack shelving delineated the exhibition space, completing the warehouse aesthetic while maintaining transparency to the fair hall.

IPPOLITO FLEITZ GROUP

highlights the luxury and independence of a classic brand with experiments in colour and texture

Zooey Braun

HG Esch

COLOGNE – Walter Knoll's iconic pieces convey a traditional sophistication with an eccentricity that speaks to the individual personalities of its owners. The German furniture maker has developed a brand architecture in recent years to convey this reputation of bold, classic and elegant independence. For the company's presentation at IMM Cologne 2017, design agency Ippolito Fleitz Group added a fresh touch to this identity, showcasing an even stronger contrarian spirit to the perceived uniformity in the industry.

The rectangular stand was organised into six scenarios by freestanding wall elements. Each of these spaces featured a radically different colour and material palette yet were united in an open sequence to form a fluid progression. The matte, monochrome textures of the walls were overlaid with softly-falling drapery and custom artworks comprising loose collages of textile fibres, lending the rooms a lived-in atmosphere. A concept specially developed for accessories featured colour-tinted acrylic glass blocks that served as backdrops for vases and bowls.

Demonstrating the craftsmanship of the brand, a separate room displayed pieces in an atelier setting and gave visitors a hands-on introduction to the upholstering process. A cafeteria formed a solid centrepiece for the exhibition, its dark, muted and enclosed tone interjected with bright velvet seating selections.

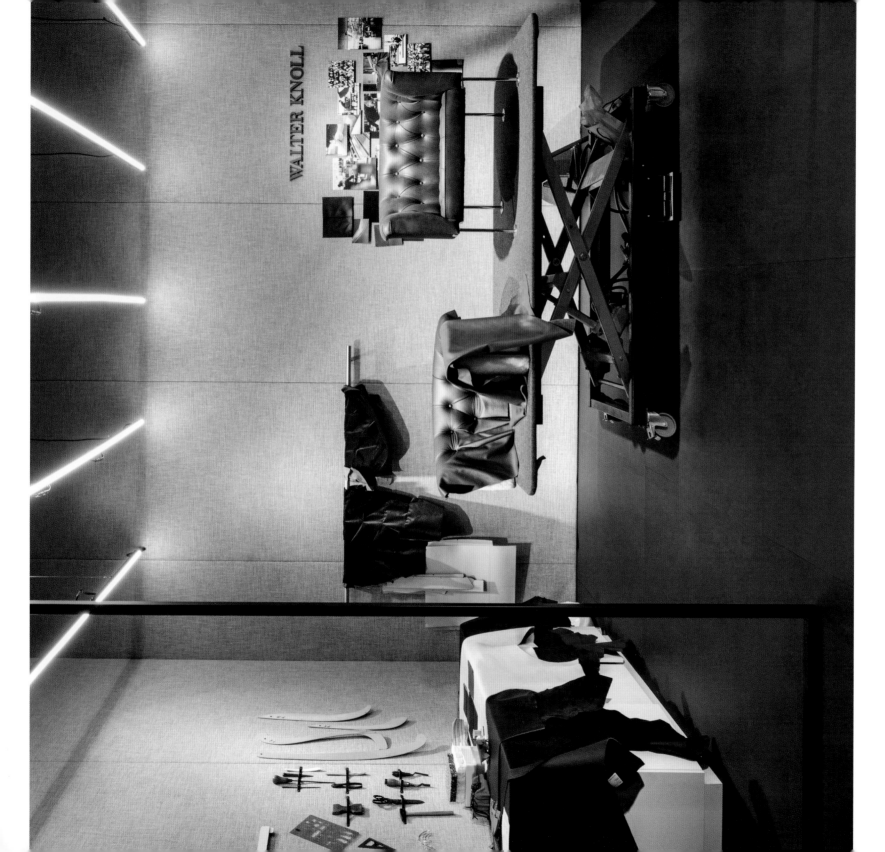

A separate room displaying pieces in an atelier setting demonstrates the brand's craftsmanship

Joachim Grothus

HG Esch

1 A podium facing out into the fair displayed a highlight product of the exhibition, the FK chair, to commemorate its 50th anniversary.

2 Full-height frames with colour transparencies were superimposed on certain walls to form vibrant abstract compositions.

TRY

OUT

The product as
a building block

PHILIPP BECK, CEO of atelier 522, shines a light on the studio's approach to brand strategy and how a company's products may become the starting point and building blocks of its stand design.

'Pushing the boundaries of products can support the story'

Your practice was established in 2007. How has the studio's approach to stand design evolved during its first decade? From the very beginning, our vision was to build stages, tell stories and create remarkable moments — something special for our clients and their clients to keep in mind.

An important dimension we have to implement in today's booth concepts is digital technology. Today the questions are: How do you want to experience the booth, physically or virtually? How do I share my experience? Yet, we do not believe in implementing digital technology just for the sake of it. It needs to generate added value. As people are increasingly faced with digital technology in their daily lives, the desire for haptic experiences rises reciprocally.

How does your approach change across product industries and young or long-time established brands? It's one approach. Together with our clients we write the play: director, main actor, secondary rolls, extras, stage props, etc. Everyone gets assigned to their role. After a strategic consultation with our clients, we design the scenery. It's not always about having the biggest booth or the loudest show. It's about being authentic, unique and telling the right story. You need to encourage the audience to join the journey, the search, and the way to success.

How do you measure the success of a stand? At the start of a project we define some important questions, on which its success is based. First and foremost, what story do we want to tell? But also, what is the client's goal? Who is the target audience; what do they need and how do we engage them most effectively? If these questions have been successfully answered and implemented, together with a multi-sensual booth experience, the story we constructed will be remembered and in that case we would say yes, then we have a successful stand. Stories help us to achieve our goals. As a powerful tool of communication, they go beyond the informative level to an emotional one. They can do what is impossible for plain information and naked figures.

Using a product as a building block of its own stand seems to me to be at once a straightforward and bold idea. What are the main advantages of this approach? The main advantage of this concept is that you can create a world around the product with all its specifications and outstanding features. The product becomes the hero of the story. Every detail from the material selection to the shape supports that hero-product. During the concept and planning phase this can be very challenging, but exciting, too. It's like a big puzzle where all the pieces need to interlock, to create the big picture. If that happens, the story can become really strong and outstanding.

How do you determine whether this is the right design approach to a project? Everything comes back to the questions asked at the start of any project, which determine and direct the storyline. In this case, what kind of product do we have? Is it physical, digital, or a service? When making a purchase decision, do customers need a selection of products to touch or look at? In the latter case, for instance, pushing the boundaries of the products through the shape and form of the display can support the story. This happens in the booth for LG Hausys by Coast Office (p 360), UNStudio's design for Mitsubishi Plastics (p 364) and many other stands in this chapter, which are entirely made of the material being shown.

Was your design for Serafini at EuroShop 2017 the first time you've followed this approach in stand design? No, in the past we've had some exhilarating booth designs using a product as a building block of its own stand. For example, a previous booth for Serafini made of mailboxes, or a booth made out of a system by the shopfitter König Ladenbau. As we are a creative agency of architects, photographers, and interior, product and graphic designers, colourful stories occur every day just because we work as an interdisciplinary team under one roof. How a booth design will look like at the end of the day always begins with the question: What story do you want to tell?

Studio Dessuant Bone

ALLAERT ALUMINIUM

Kinetic sculptures by STUDIO DESSUANT BONE demonstrate the possibilities of aluminium framing systems

KORTRIJK — As a local firm with a rich history in the city, Allaert Aluminium sought to emphasise the high-end and creative-oriented reputation of the brand for its exhibition at Kortrijk Biennale Interieur 2016. Paris-based Studio Dessuant Bone used the brand's materials to create a series of animated, interactive sculptures that carried a quietly imaginative and informative presence at the fair.

Entitled Perpetual Motion, the installation placed particular emphasis on the company's renowned Ottima low-profile frame system for guillotine windows and sliding and pivoting doors. Each of these architectural elements was transposed into an abstract kinetic object. The three pieces were framed by congruent aluminium profiles and placed in tandem with glass shutters and doors tinted in light pink and grey. The floor, finished entirely in a lighter aluminium, provided a gently reflective surface that complemented the movement of both the sculptures and visitors.

Looking down the line of sculptures from the entrance, one could watch unique forms be created by the intersection of these partitions that rotated or oscillated silently at a constant slow and meditative pace. A powerful symbol of the products' infinite architectural possibilities, the spectacle guaranteed maximum exposure at the fair and drew visitors in for a closer inspection.

JAIME PROUS ARCHITECTS
recycles a company's materials to create a dynamic and luminescent canopy

BARCELONA – A large order of aluminum profiles that was never picked up by a client became an opportunity for Alumilux & Metall-lux. The Catalan firm, specialising in aluminium, metal and glass construction solutions, commissioned Jaime Prous Architects to construct a reusable stand from the order's contents. Debuting at Construmat 2017, the installation formed an intricate, mesmerising space that revealed the materials in a bare, unprocessed state.

Suspended from the ceiling, 1800 aluminium profiles formed an undulating cape over the 108 m² floor plan. The structure rose from half a metre above a raised platform of welded steel sheets at points along the perimeter, and grew to a 5 m ceiling height towards the centre, creating an immersive, cave-like interior.

With bright halogen lights shining onto the installation from above, the profiles cast a rapturous flurry of shadows and reflections in every direction, turning the space into a complex living creature. From first encountering its exterior to losing oneself in its waves of light and void, the visitors' imagination was constantly stimulated, returning them to a childlike curiosity. Though primarily intended to showcase the company's strides in technological innovation, the structure also served as an inspiring forum for discussion and reflection.

The space beneath the structure was deliberately freed from obstructions and information to emphasise the visceral experience.

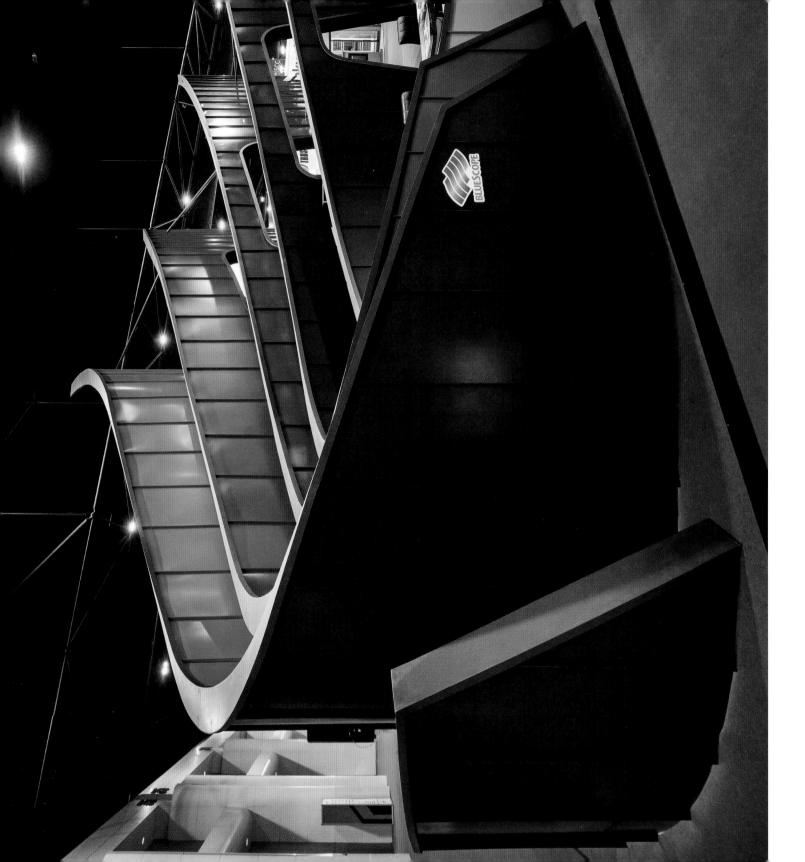

APOSTROPHYS demonstrates the agility and creative freedom of steel products with a sculptural exhibition

NONTHABURI — For its presence at Architect Expo 2017, Australian steel company BlueScope required an exhibition that would showcase the vast potential of Colorbond, its trademark product. To do so, Bangkok-based studio Apostrophys drew on an ancient and rationalistic conception of beauty – the golden spiral – which allowed the very stand's structure to illustrate the material's capabilities.

Using digital fabrication techniques and subsequent physical modelling, the team created a complex, curvilinear structure from the brand's own steel panels. Following a motion based on the golden spiral, five steel layers were placed in a concentric, radial arrangement. Each of these walls began at a height of between 4.5 and 7 m and then descended fluidly to a single meeting point at around 1 m, where the stand's information desk was placed.

While the outermost sections of the walls were lined with informative posters, the middle sections were crossed by a void that formed a continuous archway facilitating visitors' movement between each layer.

Taking on a single, vivid colour on either side, the layers formed a cool or warm colour gradient, depending on the visitors' perspective. Besides showcasing the vast range of colours in which the product is available, the gradients contributed to emphasize the fluidity of the sculptural stand.

Ketsiree Wongwan

1   The sculptural structure offered unique views from each angle: a growing curve from the front, or a continuous approach as one moved across the archway, for instance.

2   At once agile and sturdy, the structure evidenced the creative flow and flexibility that Colorbond steel afforded the designers.

E+I STUDIO takes inspiration from the Italian piazza to explore new potential in ceramic tile

ORLANDO – New York-based practice e+i studio were tapped for the Ceramics of Italy pavilion at the 2015 edition of Coverings. The team was given a 15 × 18 m rectangular floor plan that had to incorporate a café, restaurant and information desk, while showcasing a variety of Italian ceramic tiles. Inspired by the country's iconic piazzas, the space was articulated as a public space with gradual steps that doubled as seating, counters and work spaces.

These steps were created by folding the rectangular platform at the edges, resulting in inclines whose formal complexity 'is achieved with a simple system of fabrication and precise digitally generated components,' Eva Perez de Vega and Ian Gordon of e+i studio explain. The different tiles on display were water-jet cut to ensure precise interlocking patterns that allowed the stand to be assembled quickly. Conventionally perceived as a two-dimensional, orthogonal material, the tiles were displayed in more fluid and vertically-oriented arrangements, generating new perspectives on their potential use in public spaces.

The supporting structure also allowed for the mounds to be moved into different configurations. For the Orlando showcase, the 'introvert' position placed them farthest apart at diagonal corners. In the flat region between the mounds, the tile patterns were modulated in a gradient that suggested different programme zones, growing darker as they approached furniture and lighter in areas for visitor flow and access.

1 Altogether, nine different types of tile are displayed in all vertical and horizontal surfaces. Their strategic placement allowing for a gradient of colour that visually divided the different programmes.

2 A grid shell system of CNC-cut plywood ribs served as the cantilevering structure supporting the tile mounds.

E+I STUDIO encourages dynamic motion and interaction rather than stopping and gathering

CHICAGO – The Ceramics of Italy pavilion at Coverings 2016 was conceived as one of the country's lively streetscapes, favouring dynamic interactions over static gathering. The concept, once again developed by e+i studio, followed its previous goal of showcasing the nation's latest ceramic tiles in a way that explored the material's full potential.

Rather than creating a static space for gathering as booths tend to be traditionally conceived, the studio opted for a setting that would encourage dynamic interaction and movement. The 300 m² exhibition space featured two sculptural kiosks placed at opposite corners

and a winding sequence of interlocking tables running diagonally among them. Grooved and curved wood panels were stacked in a staggered configuration to shape a canopy over the kiosks, and rose in a tall, narrow spiral to form an information totem on one side of the booth. These striations created strong horizontal lines of sight that conveyed a sense of motion was furthered by the stand's colours. In fact, the tile selection for this environment intentionally took on a reduced colour palette of travertine white for the floors and deep brown for the countertops and table, shifting emphasis onto the dynamic horizontal lines.

1   Bearing the vibrant colours of the Italian flag, the totem was one exception to the minimal colour scheme, serving as a clear landmark for the larger fair space.

2   The free-form kiosk structures house the stand's main service functions of information, café and catering.

Ceramics of Italy

Ceramics of Italy

GRAND STAND 6

UNIPLAN challenges the limits of application for a chemical company's products

DUSSELDORF — Cologne-based agency Uniplan had a tall order to fill when it was commissioned to debut one of the world's leading producers of high-tech polymers, Covestro, at K 2016. With a promise of 'Pushing Boundaries', Covestro wanted to communicate its cutting-edge, innovative prowess to consumers.

Uniplan determined the ideal way to manifest this promise was to radically challenge the limits of the company's products with its exhibit design, using Covestro's own materials in ways not previously thought possible. With the assistance of the company's chemists and engineers, the firm realised a vibrant and comprehensive brand world made entirely from Covestro products.

The main attraction was a layer of curved, transparent, 6-m-high walls made from the company's polycarbonate plastic resin Makrolon. Each dyed in a single vivid hue, they formed a colour wheel representing Covestro's logo in the centre of the radial floor plan. This created a fascinating spatial experience that made the stand noticeable from a distance. Individual product displays presented the materials in a simple and haptic fashion: a bold statement of the brand's ability to make an impact through a daring use of its own products.

Uniplan realised a vibrant and comprehensive brand world made largely from Covestro products

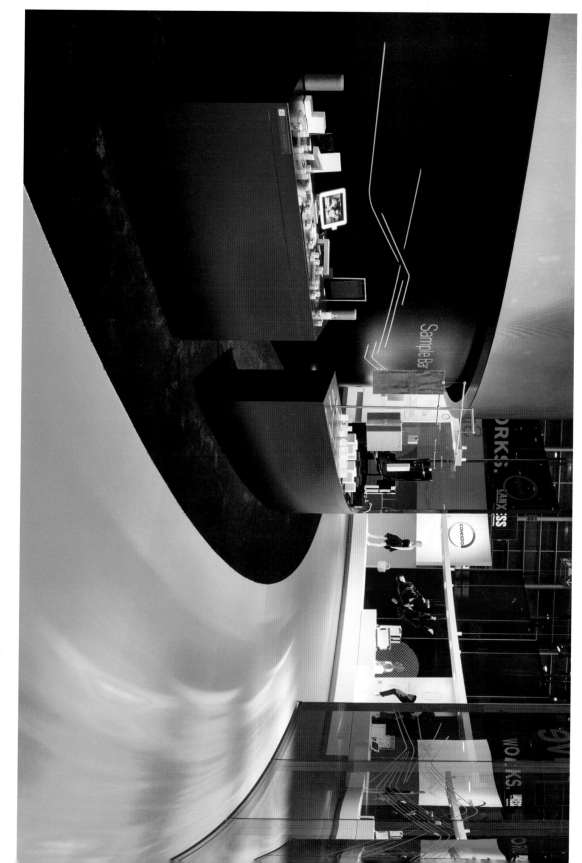

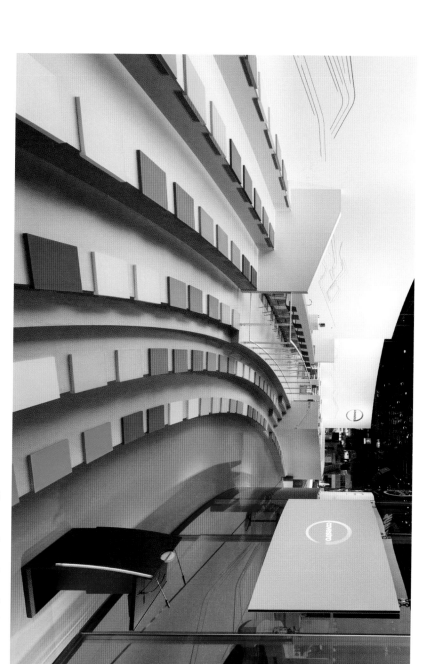

The space featured an auditorium for talks and presentations.

Pietro Savorelli

IRIS CERAMICA

AREA-17
unifies distinct
material voices
to showcase
versatility

BOLOGNA – Florence-based studio Area-17 Architecture and Interiors oversaw a monumental presence for tile producer Iris at Cersaie 2016. Inspired by mood boards, the design unified selections from each of the group's three brands – Iris Ceramica, FMG and Eiffel Gres – into a unique, relational matrix.

Opposing a curatorial preference for permeability, the booth presented itself as a secluded business lounge, whose inviting air of mystery and exclusivity promised to remove visitors from the chaos of the fair. The 300 m² horseshoe floor plan was delineated by an imposing white shell, clad in ceramic slabs featuring opulent marble veining. Dramatic, angular cuts defined its entrances.

Inside, walls and floors were also covered in white and dark grey slabs that formed a neutral backdrop for the tile display boards. These were presented as material collages and then transposed into several meeting spaces: a kitchen, an office, and informal lounges. For these areas, Area-17 paired Iris' ceramic slabs with iconic design items, as well as bespoke furnishings created from FMG materials, thus emphasising the versatility of the brand's products.

1 The marble-effect ceramic slabs cladding the exterior exemplify FMG's Marmo Calacatta Lincoln line.

2 In a meeting area, the displays were paired with luxury furniture icons such as Foscarini's Allegro lamps.

Bespoke furnishings created from FMG materials emphasise the versatility of the brand's products

esigned by

An effervescent installation by **NENDO** demonstrates the difference a simple geometric tweak can make

COLOGNE — At Orgatec 2016, international office supplies manufacturer Kokuyo presented a simple product with far-reaching implications for the workplace. 'Why not redefine the square white board as a circular structure?' was the question put forward by the product's designer Nendo. In a striking space installation, the Tokyo-based studio explored the revolutionary and multi-dimensional functionality of this proposal.

A 320 m² theatrical platform of white surfaces was interspersed with the round boards in differing colours and sizes, appearing like a cluster of overlaying dots to create a three-dimensional effervescence. Bespoke furniture including desks, benches and high counters, as well as small niches were integrated into the stand so that the new product's full potential could be demonstrated. The round boards could be rolled around freely, adapting to the motion necessary in a hectic work environment or, conversely, fixed into place as room dividers through slits cut into the furniture or the floor. They could even be used as doors to a room or shelf, or stored away in a sequence of slits carved onto the walls.

Furthering the functionality of this simple concept, the reverse sides of the boards were finished with fabric, serving as a sound absorber, while its shape is meant to challenge users to record their ideas in a radial rather than linear manner — a potential for catalysing new perspectives and thought patterns allegorized as enhancing the 'rotation' of the brain. This way, both spatially and cognitively, the circular white boards were shown to be capable of generating a more dynamic and stimulating work environment.

KVADRAT – DANSKINA

STUDIO AISSLINGER reveals the spatial and aesthetic versatility of textiles through a garden-inspired installation

COLOGNE — Danish brand Kvadrat, along with its sister brands Danskina and Kinnasand, were invited to showcase products as part of the Design Post exhibition within IMM Cologne 2016. In the hall of a former post office in Cologne, designer Werner Aisslinger created an immersive world out of the companies' textiles, generating fresh perspectives on their material capabilities.

Titled Garden of Wonders, the installation presented the textiles in a variety of vibrant and playful arrangements that spanned the entire space: laid on the floor as rugs, layered on the walls, or draped across grid construction above the display areas. The collages culminated along one wall as a series of rails where visitors could flip through a range of colours and textures. Potted plants echoed the garden theme and complemented the abundance of life in the fabrics.

The main attraction of the display, however, was a small piece of architecture dubbed by Aisslinger the 'Kvadrat cabin house'. This intimate, rectilinear volume was covered entirely in the brand's fabrics — from partitions and furniture, to louvres and shingles. Carrying a warm and bright if unusual presence in the midst of the cold German winter, the exhibit spoke cogently to the flourishing potential in the three brands' newly launched collections.

The 'Kvadrat cabin house' is covered entirely in the brand's fabrics

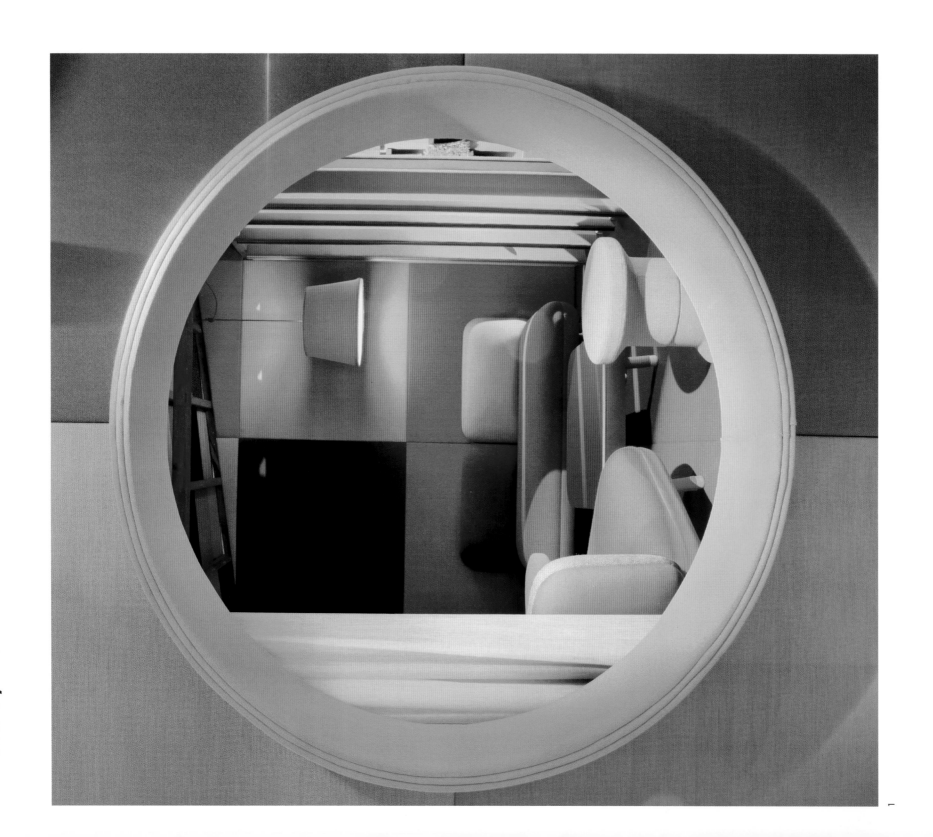

1   Stools were fashioned in the form of spools, with exposed cork along the bottom half and Kvadrat fabric covering the top half.

2   Products on display in the garden included new collections from Cristian Zuzunaga and Scholten & Baijings.

TRYOUT

David Franck

LG HAUSYS

COAST OFFICE combines form and function in a modular booth

MUNICH – For a booth to promote HI-MACS, LG Hausys called for a modular, compact and portable structure that could distinctly showcase the different features of the unique and versatile solid surface. Rather than simply displaying the material, design studio Coast Office answered to the brief by making a booth entirely of the material itself, offering an immersive, architectonic experience for visitors at BAU 2015.

The dynamic, sloping topography of the exhibit's main surface appeared to emerge seamlessly from the 25 m² base like snowdrifts, demonstrating the material's thermoforming flexibility and continuous joining capabilities. Custom, geometric fixtures in white, black, and pink were anchored amongst the white waves to form seating, tables and stands. Their angular forms contrasted with the soft, smooth curves of the plane, showcasing HI-MACS' range of texture. Translucent objects were lit within to double as light fixtures and hence suggest other functions the material could serve besides surfacing.

A glossy, black wall encompassing two sides of the square floor plan reflected the sculpture into infinity, a culmination of the material's tactile expressions of agility in an abstract and yet cogent statement of its infinite potential. Though comprising distinct modules, the booth was to be understood as a module itself that could be combined to form a vast landscape.

Rather
than simply
displaying the
product, the
stand is made
of the product
itself

LG Hausys
HI-MACS®
Natural Acrylic Stone™

COAST
OFFICE ARCHITECTURE

in collaboration with
RaumGestalten.tv
ℝℙ rosspartner

MITSUBISHI PLASTICS

UNSTUDIO showcases the potential of a material with a structure that transcends its ordinary function

MUNICH — With the success of the firm's 2015 exhibition stand design, UNStudio was commissioned again by Mitsubishi Plastics for its presence at BAU 2017. The second edition sought to extend the demonstration of the potential of their product Alpolic beyond the 2015 display. Rather than showcasing the material in the predictable form of a facade, the Amsterdam-based studio rendered it into a holistic spatial experience that transcended its function.

The stand was built up from a single proprietary structural unit inspired by geometric principles found in nature, such as the venation of leaves and the catenary lines of spider webs. By mirroring and rotating this unit, the team

constructed a fully self-supporting structure made entirely from Alpolic. The parametric design not only demonstrated the flexibility and durability of the facade material, but also allowed one to view both the fluoropolymer coating techniques of the front side and the architectural and technical anatomy of the untreated back side.

The resulting sculptural structure encapsulated a variety of different spaces for visitors to explore, including semi-enclosed areas for meetings and an information desk. Furthering the visual spectacle, pearlescent shades of pigments on the coated side created a prismatic effect that offered unique perspectives from each angle.

The coated side of the facade material was finished with FEVE fluoropolymer technology.

A resplendent installation
by **MDLAB** connects
technological advancement
with medieval inspiration

BERLIN — Samsung found the inspiration for its Quantum Dot LED television in a rather unlikely place: stained glass windows from the Middle Ages. The chlorides that medieval artists had blended with molten glass resulted in intense hues that retained their radiance for centuries. Using these nanoparticles that emit colours relative to their size — the Quantum Dot — Samsung created a television with long-lasting colours that will not fade over time.

German studio MDLab//Cheil created a vibrant installation at IFA 2016 to promote this technological breakthrough. Illustrating the inseparability of light and colour in visual experience, the exhibition juxtaposed sculptural arrangements of Quantum Dot televisions with transparent strings holding individual pieces of stained glass, lightly echoed in a white gloss floor. The glass pieces, cast in an assortment of colours, appeared to hover weightlessly in a continuum, emulating the screens' nanoparticles. Their configuration created a central point of view complemented by brilliant reflections, where visitors felt immersed in a world of dots. The curves of the television screens together formed a cavernous, three-dimensional effect and brought the particles to life with sound and visual content. Vivid, life-like footage of stained glass windows formed an immediate, emotive connection between the television and its predecessor.

MDLAB//Cheil collaborated with generative media designers schnellebuntebilder, media artist Andreas Nicolas Fischer, sound artists Kling Klang Klong and light and installation artist Christopher Bauder.

Glass dots appear to hover weightlessly in a continuum, emulating the screens' nanoparticles

SERAFINI

Merging product and display into one, ATELIER 522's design boldly towers above EuroShop 2017

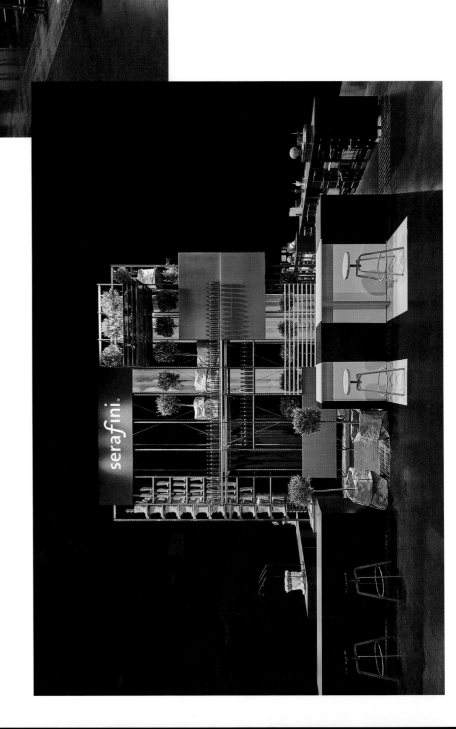

serafini.

DUSSELDORF — For the 70-year-old German retail fixture giant Serafini, the guiding question has always been how to create a harmonious connection between product and design. Long-time collaborator atelier 522 took this notion quite literally for the booth they conceived for EuroShop 2017, where the product itself served as the display.

A tower constructed entirely from Serafini's Groove modular system rose imposingly from the compact, square space, its eccentric architecture demonstrating the product's vast range of layout possibilities. Each side of the tower was equipped with partially illuminated shelving on which a myriad of objects were displayed. Ranging from apparel and sporting goods, to plants and

containers, this showcase helped demonstrate the practically unlimited versatility of the modular system for different markets. The objects also contributed to the subtle absurdism of the booth, with traffic cones serving as pendant lights and rain boots as flower vases. To bring vitality and dimension to the stand, a palette of vibrant colours was chosen for both the objects on display, and the large geometric shapes that punctuated the shelves, breaking up their linearity.

Adding to the playfulness of the stand, a spacious meeting room for business gatherings and conferences lay hidden within its curtained inner walls. Simple, rectangular counters surrounding the tower featured material samples with which visitors could interact.

The colours on each side of the tower splash onto the counters below, unifying the stand design.

Boris Demin

STUDIO DEGA explores
new architectonic
species with an updated
incarnation of their
modular exhibition system

DUSSELDORF — Studio Dega's modular, biomorphic exhibition system Infinityconst (*Grand Stand 5*, p.036–037) had already become a fixture at EuroShop, dazzling visitors each time with an ever more ambitious feat of synthesis between sculpture and light. For the 2017 fair, the St. Petersburg-based firm debuted Infinityconst Evo, a more dynamic and flexible system that enabled the quick assembly of radiant, curvilinear structures.

The Infinityconst Evo modules formed a bulbous shell around the space, as well as partitions and tunnels within. This adventurous spatial dynamic was enhanced by high-gloss floor finishes that reflected the structure. The foundational elements of the system were its stainless steel connectors, classified into four distinct categories that were printed across the floor: revolution, translation, sphere and centre. These constructors joined to form a geodesic grid of warped triangles and squares. A fabric skin stretched over the skeleton and came to life with an LED lighting system whose effects visitors could programme in real time. The result was an organic yet futuristic habitat with an infinite number of functional and aesthetic applications.

Much like what happened in previous editions, the studio shared with visitors the Infinityconst EVOCAD software used to design Infinityconst. Users were able to create their own structures and take virtual tours through their creations.

Meeting areas were furnished with iconic furniture items like Panton chairs, their curvaceous, 'space age' forms paralleling the motion of the Infinityconst Evo structure.

376   GRAND STAND 6

A fabric skin comes to life with an LED lighting system, resulting in an organic multipurpose habitat

SWAROVSKI
DESIGNERS OF THE FUTURE AWARD/
2017

JIMENEZ LAI / MARJAN VAN AUBEL / TAKT PROJECT

Marjan van Aubel /
Cyanometer

TAKT PROJECT/
Ice Crystal

JIMENEZ LAI

upcycles rejected
materials in a
modern and elegant
take on a classical
architectural form

1 Fellow award laureate Marjan Van Aubel's
   Cyanometer installation illuminated the centre
   of the exhibition, integrating solar power
   within a facetted Ilano-convex crystal
   developed by Swarovski.

2 Intense spots created heavy contrasts
   between light and dark, giving the stand a
   theatrical enigma.

3 Takt Project, the third winner of the contest,
   worked with Swarovski and a 3D printing
   company to create Ice Crystal vases, boasting
   forms not possible with traditional crystal
   glass processing.

SWAROVSKI
DESIGNERS OF THE FUTURE AWARD/
2017

JIMENEZ LAI / MARJAN VAN AUBEL / TAKT PROJECT

Freestanding structures form a cubistic deconstruction of a palazzo

BASEL — For its annual Designers of the Future Award, Swarovski invites creatives whose work spans multiple disciplines and exemplifies the technological and conceptual vanguard to develop design prototypes that utilise the company's resources. Jimenez Lai, one of the 2017 laureates, was commissioned to create the unifying structure that would showcase all winners' concepts at Design Miami/Basel.

Entitled Terrazzo Palazzo, the installation comprised a rectangular border of freestanding structures that together formed a cubistic deconstruction of the classical architectural form in its title. Lai pioneered a new terrazzo material for the construction that incorporated upcycled Swarovski crystal, referring to stones that did not pass the company's stringent quality control. By giving these otherwise wasted materials a new life, the Los Angeles-based artist highlighted Swarovski's concern with efficient use of resources.

The shapes, colours and positions of the structures symbolised the 24 hour cycle within a typical home, and the crystals were accordingly selected to embody specific elements of the day through a given colour. Additional colourways of the material were developed by Lai for each of the other winners' projects, informed by the designers' portfolios. According to Lai, 'architecture is all about telling stories. Being able to truly understand the rich history of Swarovski [...] was crucial to creating an installation that reaches both back in time, and into our future.'

MÜLLERVANTOL illustrates a furniture brand's colour and material library in a playground of spinning wheels

MILAN — In addition to its its stand at the Salone del Mobile, Vitra also took over a space near the city centre for Milan Design Week 2016. Casa Vitra hosted both a pop-up shop and installation focusing on the Vitra's Colour & Material Library, consisting of the Swiss furniture maker's developments in the use of colour, textile and material. Conceived by Amsterdam studio MüllerVanTol, Colour Machine told this aspect of the Vitra story through its classic and contemporary designs.

A series of moving mechanisms created a vibrant, playground-like setting in an open studio space. Four spinning tops oriented horizontally on the floor grouped the colours of Vitra's library into four contrasting worlds: light, dark, greens and reds. Each palette was presented as an arrangement of overlapping textiles around the upper surface of the tops. Suspended from the ceiling, nine vertically-oriented, steel-framed spinning wheels demonstrated how these colours interacted with each other, as well as with volume, shape and material. Each wheel celebrated a signature component of a Vitra design with the hues of the spectrum manifested in the corresponding palette below. Visitors were invited to spin both the tops and the wheels, allowing them to feel the textiles and forms in an interactive and playful discovery of the process of compiling the Vitra library.

Eduardo Perez

Examples of furniture components represented in the vertical colour wheels included the singular piece of the Panton chair, the base of Jean Prouvé's Em table and the shell of the Eames plastic chair.

Visitors were invited to spin the tops and wheels, allowing for an interactive and playful discovery of the process of compiling the Vitra library

Eduardo Perez

DESIGNER

INDEX

ATELIER MARKGRAPH
markgraph.de

P 194

Based in Frankfurt, Atelier Markgraph is an agency that specialises in spatial communication. An interdisciplinary design and planning provider, the atelier creates tangible experiences of companies and brands for clients all over the world. Using cutting-edge technologies, the studio develops surprising projects at the interface of business, culture and science, from exhibitions and media productions, to corporate architecture.

ATELIER MARKO BRAJOVIC
markobrajovic.com

P 210

Marko Brajovic founded his atelier in 2008 in São Paulo, and later expanded with a second office in Barcelona. The idea of the hybrid, as well as the creation of multisensorial and immersive experiences, drives the eclectic works of the multidisciplinary atelier, permeating all areas, formats and aesthetics of his projects. Its portfolio includes scenography, product design, architecture, and creative direction for a diverse global client base.

ATELIER SEITZ
atelierseitz.de

P 96, 170

For over 50 years, Atelier Seitz has been creating concepts, designing, and constructing exhibition stands, events and showrooms for clients across the globe. Its team of architects develops innovative and custom-made concepts, constantly seeking ways to reduce waste and increase recycling in trade fair projects. Working from a 4000 m² facility with over 40 qualified staff, the studio is a full-service partner for the duration of any project, from the rough sketch to project development and final touches.

AREA-17
area-17.com

P 350

Long-time friends with a shared cultural and educational background at the University of Florence, Enrico Tomidei and Andrea Iacono co-founded Area-17 in 2004. Rooted in the designers' hometown of Florence, the international firm soon opened offices in Beijing, Hong Kong, Shanghai and Cuenca, Ecuador. Area-17 is now a full service architecture and interior design studio specializing in retail, hospitality, and residential environments. By providing clients with innovative design solutions, the studio fulfills their cultural, aesthetic, operational, and marketing objectives.

Daniele de Carolis

ARIK LEVY
ariklevy.fr

P 250

Artist, technician, photographer, designer, video artist — Arik Levy's skills are multi-disciplinary and his work can be seen in prestigious galleries and museums worldwide. Best known publicly for his sculptures, installations, limited editions and design, Levy nevertheless feels that 'the world is about people, not objects.' Hailing originally from Israel, he moved to Switzerland in 1986, where he studied at Art Centre Europe and gained a distinction in Industrial Design in 1991. He currently works in his studio in Paris.

ATELIER 522
atelier522.com

P 166, 242, 372

An office for brand strategy and design, atelier 522 is always ready to undertake all possible adventures. The studio loves to explore new territories with its team of interior, product, graphic and communication designers, architects, communications specialists, business economists, artists, and philosophers. In a truly multidisciplinary environment, these specialists come together to put their energy, knowledge, talent and ideas into designing the things they dream of.

2X4
2×4.org

P 264

Founded in 1994, 2×4 is a global design consultancy headquartered in New York City with satellite studios in Madrid and Beijing. The studio's work focuses on brand strategy for cultural and commercial clients who value the power of design. The team identifies and clarifies core institutional values and creates innovative, experiential, participatory and visually-dynamic ways to engage key audiences worldwide. 2×4's intellectual and creative conviction is that thoughtful design can make an essential contribution to every level of cultural discourse. Clients include Arper, Nike and Prada.

ALESSANDRA DALLOLI
alessandradalloli.it

P 274

Alessandra Dalloli graduated from the Polytechnic University of Milan in 1994 and started her own architectural practice in 2001. She specialises in showroom and store design, fair stands and private residential interior design. Customer care and attention to detail are the main values that characterise Dalloli's work. In her projects, the designer always seeks out the most creative and innovative architectural solutions, in combination with aesthetic research.

APOSTROPHYS
apostrophys.com

P 30, 340

Apostrophys is a marketing agency that specialises in brand communication by means of an integrated design approach based on user behaviour and interaction with various media and the built environment. The full-service studio provides product, graphic and communication designers, architects, communications specialists, business economists, artists, and philosophers. In a truly multidisciplinary environment, these specialists come together to put their energy, knowledge, talent and ideas into designing the things they dream of.

ATELIER TSUYOSHI TANE
at-ta.fr

Atelier Tsuyoshi Tane Architects is a multi-disciplinary, international atelier practicing architecture, design, urbanism and space design. Based in Paris, the studio has completed projects throughout Europe, Asia and North America.

BLACKSPACE
black.space

An international and owner-managed design company based in Munich, Blackspace has supported brands and companies in the areas of strategy, branding, experience and motion for over 30 years. Named after and driven by a will to 'make the incomprehensible tangible and give shape to the unimaginable,' the firm stands for top-quality design and unique brand experiences, whether analogue, digital, or virtual. The studio operates from the belief that it is possible to develop strong, long-lasting relationships between clients and brands through extraordinary, unforgettable experiences.

C&C DESIGN
cocopro.cn

C&C Design was founded in Guangzhou by design director and senior interior architect Peng Zheng in 2005. The studio's name, short for Cooperate and Coexist, determines and embodies its spirit of compatibility, providing clients a one-stop service for project planning, architecture and interior design. C&C has established long-term relationships with companies such as Poly, Vanke, Midea Group, Lai Fung and CapitaLand. Its work has garnered many international accolades, including the iF Gold, Red Dot, and Interior Design's Best of Year.

BASIS DESIGNSTUDIO
hallobasis.com

Basis Designstudio was founded by Felix Vorbeck and Johannes Winkler in early 2017 after the success of their Let's Make The Office Great Again project. Vorbeck and Winkler have been working together since they began studying communication design at the University of Applied Sciences Mainz, subsequently collaborating on a master's thesis at the University of Applied Sciences Dusseldorf. The two designers use their expertise in typography and editorial design to create unique and sustainable access to brands, products, events and information.

BLOCHER PARTNERS
blocherpartners.com

Since 1989, Blocher Partners has created opportunities and developed ideas to connect experiences and make spaces happen: spaces of action. Aware that space is not an empty container but a product of social activities, the team focuses its multi-disciplinary research and practice on three main cultural aspects: social, trade, and communication. The firm was founded by Dieter and Jutta Blocher in Stuttgart, Germany. Today, it employs over 160 staff across three offices in Germany and India.

CALVI BRAMBILLA
calvibrambilla.it

Tommaso Sartori

Calvi Brambilla was founded in Milan in 2006 by Fabio Calvi and Paolo Brambilla. Having met at the Polytechnic University of Milan during their undergraduate studies, the two designers went their separate ways before deciding to establish a collaborative studio. A multidisciplinary firm, their work encompasses architecture, interior design and product design.

BENZ & ZIEGLER
b-and-z.com

Benz & Ziegler operates in the fields of architecture, brand architecture and interior design. The practice was established in 2012 by Matthias Benz and Christoph Ziegler. Both founders gained extensive international experience at major architecture firms before setting up their own studio in Munich. Benz & Ziegler has a special interest in transitions in architecture, with a focus on closing the missing links between architecture and interior design.

BRAUNWAGNER
braunwagner.de

Braunwagner is a design agency that focuses on environmental, product and communication design, as well as architecture and consulting for strategic brand development. Since its foundation in Aachen in 1999, the firm expanded in 2013 with a second office in Berlin. Led by Manfred Wagner and Marina Franke, the 25-strong creative team emotionalises corporate identities and transforms brand values into spatial communication, with creativity, know-how and enthusiasm.

COAST OFFICE
coastoffice.de

Coast Office is a multidisciplinary design practice active internationally in the fields of architecture, interiors and exhibitions. Founded and directed by Zlatko Antolovic and Alexander Wendlik in 2005, its core focus is to develop architecture and spaces that engage all senses and foster interaction between people, space and technology. Its diverse portfolio is the result of a conceptual approach that explores history, culture, nature, society and brand identities to find a specific solution for each client.

FERRUCCIO LAVIANI
laviani.com

P 288, 290

Ferruccio Laviani's work focuses mainly on product and interior design, art direction and graphics. Since 1991, he has served as the art director for Kartell and has played the same role for other companies. Among his clients are Cassina, Missoni, Citroen, Ermenegildo Zegna, Zara and Samsung. Many of his products have been featured in museums and shows internationally, including two pieces on display in the permanent collection of the Indianapolis Museum of Art.

FÖRSTBERG LING
forstbergling.com

P 224

Förstberg Ling is an office for architecture and design established in 2015 and based in Malmö, Sweden. Its founding partners, Björn Förstberg and Michael Ling, first met at Lund School of Architecture, from which they graduated in 2010. The studio's projects range from small interiors and furniture to larger buildings, always with a focus on detailing and materiality.

FRANCESC RIFÉ
rife-design.com

P 256

Interior and industrial designer Francesc Rifé founded his studio in Barcelona in 1994 and currently leads a team of professionals from several design fields. His work is influenced by minimalism and follows a tradition of craftsmanship, focusing on ways of approaching spatial order and geometric proportion, with a special attraction for fine materials. Rifé has received numerous accolades from Contract World, Emporia, Red Dot, FAD and the 8th Ibero-American Biennial CIDI of Interior Design.

E+I STUDIO
eistudio.net

P 342, 344

Founded in 2010 by partners Eva Perez de Vega and Ian Gordon, e+i studio is an architecture and design practice based in New York. The atelier engages in projects of all scales, from public infrastructure and residential renovations, to exhibition, set and product design. Informed by a background in movement-based expression, the team approaches architecture as an interdisciplinary practice that emerges from the exploration of the performance of matter and bodies in space.

EINSZU33
einszu33.com

P 38, 122

Established in 1999, einszu33 is an international practice for corporate architecture, brand communication and interior design which develops distinct concepts for interiors and space staging. Co-directors Hendrik Müller and Georg Thiersch lead a team of 10 from the Munich-based office. Award-winning projects feature the design of showrooms, retail stores, exhibition stands, office environments and concepts for hospitality. Einszu33 works for renowned companies in varying sectors with clients including Aesop, Beko and Gaggenau.

ERCO
erco.com

P 118

Founded in 1934, Erco is a leading international specialist in architectural lighting and LED technology. The company, based in Ludenscheid, now operates as a global player with independent sales organisations and partners in 55 countries. Since 2015, Erco's portfolio is 100 percent LED, developing and producing digital luminaires with a focus on photometry, electronics and design. Erco understands digital light as the fourth dimension of architecture and strives to provide highly precise, efficient lighting solutions to support creative designers in realising their visions.

D'ART DESIGN GRUPPE
d-art-design.de

P 22, 104, 168

D'art Design Gruppe, a firm specializing in spatial communication, was established in 1991. The studio's approach is one in which creative design skills merge with interdisciplinary expertise. Headquartered in Neuss, Germany with a second office in Seoul, Dart works in the field of retail and exhibition design for global clients, with a focus on strategic consulting and conceptual development of brand and corporate appearances.

DESIGNPLUS
designplus.org

P 202

Designplus is an agency for spatial brand communication. The German studio sees itself as an interdisciplinary agency, representing brands in the fashion and luxury goods sector in a cross-channel manner and with a lasting fascination. Designplus supports its customers with brand consulting and communication, spatial staging, individual object manufacturing, as well as international serial production. Founded in 1995 by Gaby Krauss and Peter Gross, today more than 40 employees develop unmistakable brand production on all channels.

DIMORESTUDIO
dimorestudio.eu

P 278

Founded in Milan in 2003 by Britt Moran and Emiliano Salci, Dimore studio is a full-service, global architectural and design studio. Its work spans residential, retail and hospitality interior design projects, as well as furniture, textile and lighting design. From the outset, Dimore studio's vision of bold, unexpected, colour-saturated design and the creation of richly alloyed and layered atmospheres, set the firm apart. The studio's clients include Fendi, Aesop, Pomellato, Frette and Boglioli.

Luke Hayes

LEE BROOM
leebroom.com

P 300

As one of the UK's leading product designers, Lee Broom has created over 100 furniture, accessory and lighting designs across 16 collections since 2007. Broom has also designed products and interiors for other leading global brands, including Christian Louboutin, Mulberry and Wedgwood, alongside over 45 retail, restaurant and bar interiors. Changing materials and silhouettes from season to season, as a designer he strives to embrace and explore new themes whilst still keeping an overarching style.

KING GEORGE
kinggeorge.land

P 14

King George was founded in 2010 by Nicolas Block, who now serves as the creative director of the company. Headquartered in Sint-Niklaas and with an office in Amsterdam, the studio comprises 22 employees working in the fields of installation, interior and graphic design, and PR. 'The mad creative agency,' as it describes itself, specialises in not only creating stories, but also bringing them to life in a highly innovative, experiential ways. Clients include Nestlé, Coca-Cola, Alessi and Whirlpool.

JIMENEZ LAI
bureau-spectacular.net

P 378

Jimenez Lai works in the world of art, architecture and education and is the founder of Bureau Spectacular, a group of individuals who practice architecture through the contemplation of art, history, politics, sociology, linguistics, mathematics, graphic design, technology and storytelling. Lai is widely exhibited and published around the world, with accolades including the Architectural League Prize for Young Architects and the Debut Award at the Lisbon Triennale.

MDLAB
mdlab.cheil.com

P 368

Based in Schwalbach am Taunus in Germany, MDLab//Cheil Germany is a design agency focusing on brand spaces. The team consists of 20 international creative individuals working together on a large variety of projects, including global trade fairs, museums, corporate events and retail solutions. The inspiration for the studio's work comes from data, art, technology and design trends. With an interdisciplinary approach, MDLab always aims to create concepts that go beyond the ordinary.

KNOBLAUCH
knoblauch.eu

P 48

Knoblauch was founded in 1909 by Fidel Knoblauch as a small, family-owned carpentry workshop. Three generations later, the company's specialties expanded to shop fitting systems for high-profile retailers like Polo Ralph Lauren. In the last decade, under the auspices of current owner Juergen Zahn, Knoblauch has become an international design studio. With over 200 employees, Knoblauch develops and builds furnishing concepts for brands, retailers and restaurants. Clients include Hugo Boss, Swatch, Lacoste and Saturn Connect.

JOHANNA MEYER-GROHBRÜGGE
meyer-grohbruegge.com

P 268

Johanna Meyer-Grohbrügge is an architect, designer and teacher who lives and works in Berlin. The work of her practice Büro Johanna Meyer-Grohbrügge and joint office June14 Meyer-Grohbrügge & Chermayeff ranges from large-scale projects, to trade fair designs, and building renovations. Meyer-Grohbrügge has taught at Columbia GSAAP and Münster School of Architecture, is a guest professor at DIA in Dessau and leads the Berlin Studio of Washington University St. Louis.

MÜLLERVANTOL
mullervantol.nl

P 382

MüllerVanTol is an Amsterdam-based studio for industrial and interior design headed by Christiane Müller and Bas van Tol. The studio's aim is to make places of excellent quality, designing interiors and materials to the highest standards. With complementary backgrounds in product and spatial design, the team creates site-specific and custom-made workspaces, exhibitions and hospitality venues. MüllerVanTol also develops colour and material concepts and surface materials for leading manufacturers in the international contract market.

KRISTOF PYCKE
kreon.com

P 228

Born in Belgium, Kristof Pycke graduated from the Henry Van De Velde Institute in Antwerp in 1995. Three years later, he joined the product development team at lighting manufacturer Kreon and is today the art director of the company. Following the belief that architects don't need lighting appliances, but light, atmosphere and comfort, Kreon's designs enter into dialogue with architecture as an equal partner.

JYSK DISPLAY
jyskdisplay.com

P 322

Since 1970, Jysk Display has created world-class trade fair stands for a wide range of industries. As Northern Europe's largest supplier of trade fair stands — producing over 700 a year — the studio controls every link in the value chain from its own production facilities at Viborg, Denmark. Jysk Display currently works with over 70 clients, including Biamp Systems, Vestas, Fibervision and Bang & Olufsen.

MUTABOR
mutabor.de

P 12, 110, 116

Meaning 'I'm going to change' in Latin, Mutabor was founded by Johannes Plass and Heinrich Paravicini in Hamburg in 1998. The studio works strategically and creatively in the design, architecture and experience sectors with a mission to help brands establish a stronger, more sustainable impact and a better culture through the power of their identity. Clients include Audi, Bosch, Bundesliga, Daimler and Deutsche Telekom.

NORMAL ARHITEKTURA
normal.ba

P 180

Founded in Bosnia and Herzegovina in 2006 by partners Emir Salkić and Muhamed Serdarević, normal arhitektura first came to public attention with its designs for the FedEx headquarters in Sarajevo and the Music Farm recording studio in Ilidza, as well as modular, prefabricated housing systems used in residential buildings in Switzerland and Germany. The team of five architects is currently working on a number of projects both nationally and across Europe.

OFFICE
officekgdvs.com

P 190

OFFICE was founded in 2002 by Kersten Geers and David Van Severen. The studio is renowned for its idiosyncratic architecture, in which utopian and non-realised projects are also customary. The team does not pretend to invent architecture, but rather reflects and considers what it can signify and be today, reducing the discipline to its bare essence. The studio won the Venice Biennale Silver Lion for most promising young architect in 2010, and the Belgian Prize for Architecture in 2009, 2013 and 2015.

NENDO
nendo.jp

P 354

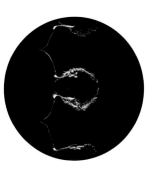

Joakim Blockstrom

Nendo was founded by its chief designer Oki Sato in 2002. The studio currently has offices in Tokyo and Milan, and its service offerings span numerous fields, including product, interior and graphic design, architecture and exhibitions. Major clients include Louis Vuitton, Camper, Haagen-Dazs, Boffi, Cappellini, Flos, Victoria & Albert Museum and Fritz Hansen.

NORMANN COPENHAGEN
normann-copenhagen.com

P 308

Normann Copenhagen is a Danish design company with a mission to create original and innovative products that withstand the test of time. Established in 1999 by Jan Andersen and Poul Madsen, the brand encompasses a wide and continuously growing collection of furniture, lighting, textiles and home accessories. Its own design studio develops product, furniture, space and fair designs for the brand. Normann Copenhagen's stand at Salone 2016 was developed by in-house designer Hans Hornemann, who graduated from the University of Aalborg with a Master of Engineering in 2014.

PALOMBA SERAFINI ASSOCIATI
palombaserafini.com

P 296

Enrico Costantini

Ludovica and Roberto Palomba founded Palomba Serafini Associati in Milan in 1994. The studio's goal is to design free projects that interact in an evident and immediate way with clients. Numerous accolades such as the Compasso D'Oro and the Red Dot, Design Plus and German Design awards attest to the prestige of its work. Palomba Serafini's current projects include residential architecture and contract, interior and yacht design projects worldwide.

NONE COLLECTIVE
none.business

P 128

None Collective is an artistic collective based in Rome that was founded in 2015 by Gregorio De Luca Comandini, Mauro Pace and Saverio Villirillo. The team of nearly 20 people comprises artists, architects, photographers, interior, graphics and sound designers, and visual artists that work together along the boundaries of architecture, design and technological research. The atelier's factory model setting and multi-disciplinary team allow for the development of unique, cutting edge, high quality ideas and technical solutions that use internal resources in every facet of the work, from concept to realisation.

O/M LIGHT
om-light.com

P 238

Established as a brand in 2012, O/M traces its origins to more than 50 years of experience in manufacturing lighting fixtures. O/M's team is involved throughout the cycle of design, development and sale. While turning to the greatest specialists in the world to remain at the forefront, O/M has a highly competent specialist staff of its own working in multidisciplinary teams who ensure the efficient management needed to create the tools for great lighting design.

PAOLO CESARETTI
paolocesaretti.it

P 132, 244, 248

Paolo Cesaretti is a design consultant and art director who explores the concept of designed space as a communication tool. His practice specialises in exhibition and retail design and brand identity, particularly on innovation and research. Clients include companies from diverse fields including manufacturing and trade, mass-market retailing, digital media, finance and communication. He is also a lecturer at the Scuola Politecnica di Design Milano and guest professor at the Domus Academy and Politecnico di Milano.

SCHMIDHUBER
schmidhuber.de

P 12, 80, 110

Established in 1984, Schmidhuber is a Munich-based design studio that specialises in brand-specific architectural solutions. With a team of over 70 architects and interior designers, the studio implements visionary concepts and moving brand experiences for trade shows, exhibitions, events, shops and showrooms. Openness, respect and reliability are the main pillars of the studio's successful cooperation with its international client base, fostering a refreshing approach to each new project.

Lutz Sternstein

SEBASTIAN HERKNER
sebastianherkner.com

P 140

Sebastian Herkner was born in 1981 and studied product design at the Offenbach University of Art and Design, focusing on designing objects and furniture that merge various cultural contexts and combine new technologies with traditional craftsmanship. Since founding his own design studio in Offenbach am Main in 2006, he has worked on interior design projects for exhibitions and museums, and designed myriad products for manufacturers such as Fontana Arte, Cappellini, Moroso, Pulpo and Rosenthal.

SIMPLE
simple.de

P 16, 120

Simple specialises in spatial and media communication. Staged spatial experiences such as exhibition booths and showrooms are as important a part of its portfolio as multimedia interactions and virtual spaces. With a core team of 20 and a large network of specialists, the Cologne and Berlin-based firm serves clients from industry, business and the public sector. Felix Hansen and Andreas Salsamendi have been the company's managing partners since its foundation in 2000.

Ibai Acevedo

RAMÓN ÚBEDA
ramonubeda.com

P 270

Ramón Úbeda started working in the world of design in 1984 and has since then toiled on all fronts in the field: as journalist, graphic designer, designer, art director and curator. Out of his broad portfolio of professional activity, he feels most at ease working within companies as a consultant and art director. Úbeda performs this role in some of the most important Spanish design companies, including BD Barcelona Design, Camper, Metalarte, Andreu World and Zuzunaga.

RAUMKONTOR
raumkontor.com

P 280

Founded in 1993 by Andrea Weitz and Jens Wendland, Raumkontor is a transdisciplinary team of interior designers, architects and media designers. While this diverse set of skills allows for a varied spectrum of projects, holistic spatial concepts, tailor-made designs and innovative, functional structures ensure the quality and longevity of the end result. The agency's award-winning fair stands tell vibrant stories with catchy and inspiring display concepts.

SCHEMATA ARCHITECTS
schemata.jp

P 324

Jo Nagasaka was born in Osaka and brought up in the Chiba prefecture of Japan. He studied architecture at Tokyo National University of Fine Arts and Music and, after graduating, he established the office Schemata Architects. Since 2007, the studio has been based in Tokyo from where an ever-expanding portfolio covers projects such as residential and retail interiors, exhibition stands and art installations, hotels and public institutions.

PETER SCHMIDT GROUP
peter-schmidt-group.de

P 72

Currently one of the top brand communication and design agency in Germany, Peter Schmidt Group has been leading brands to success for over 40 years. The studio effectively combines strategic consultancy with excellent design, brand implementation and management. With clients like Hilti, Linde and Sennheiser, the agency's portfolio ranges from retail, pop-up spaces and trade fairs, to event design and digitally-interconnected and interactive brand communication.

PIERRE CHARPIN
pierrecharpin.com

P 314

Pierre Charpin started his own practice in 1990. The atelier is located in the Paris suburb of Ivry-sur-Seine. His work spans industrial products, objects in limited editions, drawings and scenographies. The studio's major clients include Galerie Kreo, Alessi, Hermès, Hay, Ceramiche Piemme and Ligne Roset.

POR VOCAÇÃO
porvocacao.com

P 238

What started as a premium clothing store back in 1997 is now an accomplished creative and marketing studio, committed to making companies and brands effectively communicate with their target audiences and achieve sales. Defined by a distinctively creative and marketing-rooted approach, Porto-based Por Vocação works with a clear strategic vision that respects each client's core values.

UEBERHOLZ
ueberholz.de

P 88, 126

Established in 1987, Ueberholz is led by architect and communication designer Nico Ueberholz. The firm is fascinated by creating places for encounters, with the aim of establishing and supporting processes of communication. With expertise in the fields of trade fair and exhibition design, Ueberholz also develops concepts for event services, retail construction and music architecture.

UNIPLAN
uniplan.com

P 42, 272, 346

Founded in 1960, Uniplan is a leading agency for brand communication, focusing on bringing together people and brands. A team of 600 experts employed across 9 branches worldwide creates brand promotions for events, trade fairs, showrooms and road shows. Uniplan's clients include renowned companies such as Adidas, Daimler, Toshiba and ZDF.

Inga Powilleit

UNSTUDIO
unstudio.com

P 34, 364

Ben van Berkel studied architecture at the Rietveld Academy in Amsterdam and at the Architectural Association in London, receiving the AA Diploma with Honours in 1987. In 1988, he and Caroline Bos set up an architectural practice in Amsterdam, extending their theoretical and writing projects to the practice of architecture. UNStudio presents itself as a network of specialists in architecture, urban development and infrastructure. The firm has a staff of over 200 creatives from 27 countries, with office locations in Amsterdam, Shanghai and Hong Kong.

TEAMLAB
teamlab.art

P 44

Founded in 2001 by Toshiyuki Inoko, teamLab is an interdisciplinary art collective that brings together professionals from various fields of practice: artists, programmers, engineers, CG animators, mathematicians, architects, graphic designers and editors. Referring to themselves as 'ultratechnologists', the group aims to transcend the boundaries between art, science, technology and creativity through co-creative activities.

TISCH 13
tisch13.com

P 186

Since its foundation in 2001, Tisch 13 has been creating distinctive, multi-dimensional brand communication. The Munich-based design agency is managed by owner Heidi Bücherl. Its two creative masterminds, Pat Kalt and Carsten Röhr, are both members of ADC Deutschland and have received many prestigious awards for their work. The firm's recipe for success is a passionate, cross-media orientation and an unrivalled feeling for new design and communication opportunities and trends.

TRIAD BERLIN
triad.de

P 294

As a creative agency focusing on spatial communication, Triad Berlin has been designing and producing exhibitions, museums, theme parks, trade fairs, brand environments, retail spaces and events across the globe since 1994. Founder and CEO Prof. Lutz Engelke calls his company a 'think and do tank'. With offices in Berlin and Shanghai, Triad pools the technical and creative expertise of more than 200 people and constantly breaks new ground at the intersection of science, culture and economics.

STUDIO JOANNA LAAJISTO
joannalaajisto.com

P 8

Studio Joanna Laajisto is a Helsinki-based boutique design agency founded in 2010. The team works in the field of commercial interiors, including retail, hospitality and workplace design, as well as product and concept design. Based on the belief that a well-designed project is the best form of sustainability, the studio crafts its designs following a thorough understanding of its clients' needs and the interiors' purposes. Clients include Vitra, Cecil and fellow Helsinki-based hospitality company We Are Group.

Arjan Benning

STUDIO RODERICK VOS
roderickvos.nl

P 318

Founded by Claire and Roderick Vos in 1995, Studio Roderick Vos is an interdisciplinary design team of 5 creatives based in Heusden, Belgium. Specialising in the fields of textile, furniture and industrial design, the agency has worked with such prestigious clients as Moooi, Linteloo, Pode and Cor Unum. The studio's approach to design defies the norm of simply giving a manufacturer a design with which to work, instead building up a complete brand.

Stefano De Monte

STUDIO VALENTINA FOLI
valentinafolli.com

P 150, 304

Valentina Folli is a passionate designer with an all-around approach, combining strategic product and spatial design with branding and communication. She founded her studio in 2010 in Milan. Since then, she has been working across design disciplines: crafting brand architecture for Nemo lighting, curating re-editions for Le Corbusier and Charlotte Perriand, realising interior and styling projects for Cappellini and designing new luxury packaging materials for Icma. In 2013, Foli established virtual design studio UNA.works.

VITAMIN E
vitamin-e.com

P 154

An agency under the Hamburg-based Vertikom Group, Vitamin E has developed unique forms of spatial brand communication since 1998. As a studio for live communications, its team of 30 thinks and works in an interdisciplinary, multi-dimensional and often unusual manner. Through synchronised cooperation between the disciplines of design, architecture, events and exhibitions, Vitamin E has developed holistic communication solutions for clients such as Olympus, Opel and Vodafone.

WHITEVOID
whitevoid.com

P 90

Whitevoid operates at the crossovers between art, design, architecture and technology. Founded in 2004 by Christopher Bauder, the multidisciplinary studio realises large-scale art and design pieces and environments. The studio comprises specialists in interaction, media and product design as well as interior architecture and electronic engineering. Its projects focus on the translation of bits and bytes into objects and environments and vice versa. Space, object, sound and interaction form key elements of all works.

VXLAB
vxlab.org

P 212, 284

Founded in 2007 in Castellón, Spain, VXLab is a staunch defender of critical thinking as the core for great design management. The team, comprising professionals from all areas of branding and design, delivers strategic and business-oriented solutions for projects whose fields range from art direction, editorial and interior design, to ephemeral installations and product development, to name a few.

WALBERT-SCHMITZ
walbert-schmitz.de

P 114

Walbert-Schmitz was established in 1966 and is a family-owned company based in Aachen. Specialising in exhibition and stand construction, the firm offers a wide range of expertise in the field of three-dimensional brand communication: strategy, conception, design and architecture, as well as in production, installation and dismantling. The company employs more than 100 members of staff and maintains worldwide partnerships with specialised suppliers.

EVENT

INDEX

CREDITS

GRAND STAND 6
Designing Stands for Trade Fairs and Events

PUBLISHER
Frame

EDITOR
Ana Martins

AUTHORS
Evan Jehl (projects) and Ana Martins (interviews)

GRAPHIC DESIGNER
Zoe Bar-Pereg (Frame)

PREPRESS
Edward de Nijs

COVER PHOTOGRAPHY
None Collective

PRINTING
IPP Printers

TRADE DISTRIBUTION USA AND CANADA
Consortium Book Sales & Distribution, LLC.
34 Thirteenth Avenue NE, Suite 101
Minneapolis, MN 55413-1007
T +1 612 746 2600
T +1 800 283 3572 (orders)
F +1 612 746 2606

TRADE DISTRIBUTION BENELUX
Frame Publishers B.V.
Luchtvaartstraat 4
1059 CA Amsterdam
the Netherlands
distribution@frameweb.com
frameweb.com

TRADE DISTRIBUTION REST OF WORLD
Thames & Hudson Ltd
181A High Holborn
London WC1V 7QX
United Kingdom
T +44 20 7845 5000
F +44 20 7845 5050

ISBN: 978-94-92311-19-1

© 2018 Frame Publishers, Amsterdam, 2018

The Koninklijke Bibliotheek lists this publication in the Nederlandse Bibliografie: detailed bibliographic information is available on the internet at http://picarta.pica.nl

Printed on acid-free paper produced from chlorine-free pulp. TCF ∞
Printed in Poland

987654321